Selected Poems of
Garcilaso de la Vega

A BILINGUAL EDITION

Selected Poems of
GARCILASO DE LA VEGA

Edited and Translated by John Dent-Young

The University of Chicago Press :: Chicago and London

JOHN DENT-YOUNG is a freelance editor and translator who has also translated from Chinese and was a lecturer in English at the Chinese University of Hong Kong for nearly twenty years. His most recent book, *Selected Poems of Luis de Góngora: A Bilingual Edition* (2007), also published by the University of Chicago Press, won the Premio Valle Inclán Translation Prize of the Society of Authors (UK).

The University of Chicago Press, Chicago 60637
The University of Chicago Press, Ltd., London
© 2009 by The University of Chicago
All rights reserved. Published 2009
Printed in the United States of America

18 17 16 15 14 13 12 11 10 09   1 2 3 4 5

ISBN-13: 978-0-226-14188-6   (cloth)
ISBN-10: 0-226-14188-8   (cloth)

Library of Congress Cataloging-in-Publication Data

Vega, Garcilaso de la, 1503–1536.
    [Poems. English & Spanish. Selections]
    Selected poems of Garcilaso de la Vega : a bilingual edition / edited and
translated by John Dent-Young.
        p. cm.
    Includes bibliographical references and index.
    ISBN-13: 978-0-226-14188-6 (cloth : alk. paper)
    ISBN-10: 0-226-14188-8 (cloth : alk. paper) 1. Spanish poetry—Classical period,
1500–1700. I. Dent-Young, John. II. Title.
    PQ6391.A5D45 2009
    861'.3—dc22
                                                                    2008053315

♾ The paper used in this publication meets the minimum requirements of the American National Standard for Information Sciences—Permanence of Paper for Printed Library Materials, ANSI Z39.48-1992.

Contents

SONGS
Introduction   57

ELEGIES AND EPISTLE TO BOSCÁN
Introduction   75

ECLOGUES

Introduction   117

Title page of the first edition of the works of Boscán and Garcilaso (1543).

Introduction

To anyone interested in Spanish literature, Garcilaso de la Vega needs little introducing. Ever since his poems were first published in 1543, seven years after his death, he has been one of Spain's most popular and critically acclaimed poets. Given that his poetry is the reverse of popular, in the more technical sense of the word, being inspired by literary and foreign models, the popularity would seem surprising if we ignored his biography. He has all the attributes of a romantic hero: noble, brave, cultured, apparently modest and without affectation, the personification of the ideal courtier proposed by Castiglione in *The Book of the Courtier*, a book he was instrumental in getting translated into Spanish. He served the emperor Charles V well, fighting in at least four campaigns, in two of which he was wounded, and carrying out important diplomatic missions. He was present at some of the major political events of his time. He died at the age of thirty-six, or thereabouts, in a military action. He knew Latin and Greek, French and Italian, and met some of the most important contemporary writers and intellectuals. He had a number of love affairs but, in the popular conception, just one true love, the woman who inspired his best poetry and was, fortunately for Spanish literature, unattainable. He even suffered punishment for what might appear to be a minor indiscretion and accepted it stoically. And as if all this were not enough, he changed the course of Spanish literature.

The chief innovation was the introduction into Spanish of the verse forms of the Italians, their sonnets and canzoni, their terza rima and ottava rima and above all the hendecasyllable.[1] Also some of the content comes from Italy, in the form of myths and rhetorical elements derived from Greek and Roman literature. It was a joint project in which Garcilaso's friend Boscán took the lead, with some prompting from the Venetian ambassador to the Spanish court, Andrea Navagero. An idea of what they saw as a civilizing mission to redeem the barbarity of Spanish literature can be had from the Garcilaso letter that served as a preface to Boscán's translation of *The Book of the Courtier* (see appendix B). Their poetry was first published posthumously by Boscán's widow, as "The works of Boscán, and some by Garcilaso, in four volumes." Although Garcilaso began as junior partner in the enterprise, his poetry outshone his friend's, and some thirty years later began to be published on its own, with enthusiastic commentaries, in 1569 by the Salamancan scholar known as El Brocense and by the Seville poet Fernando de Herrera in 1580.

If the traditional account is not completely satisfactory, it is not because facts are disputed, although some are. The problem, as with most heroic legends, is that it makes it all seem too easy. A modern reader may want to ask questions. How, for example, can a few love sonnets and some imitative pastoral verse qualify their author for such renown? Today, the Nobel prize committee would surely have reservations about so narrow an output. Or, how can there be such a gap between the different sides of Garcilaso's life? It is not just a difficulty in understanding how someone can be poet, soldier, and courtier all at the same time, taking up, as Garcilaso himself put it, "now the pen and now the sword." There is precedent for this, in Elizabethan England or Renaissance Italy; and Garcilaso, after all, was involved in his friend Boscán's translation into Spanish of Castiglione's book, which desires the courtier to be supremely versatile. What does

---

1. The introduction of Italian meters is not the only story to be told about Spanish poetry. As important and perhaps more unique is the survival and enduring prestige of popular forms like the romance or ballad. But that is not Garcilaso's story.

not accord well with our modern desire for authenticity is that a man of action, engaged as Garcilaso was in important and dangerous activities, should write largely of the loves of shepherds. Reason tells us, though Garcilaso does not, that an important element in his life was the need to survive hazardous journeys by land and sea, hand-to-hand fighting in Spain, France, and North Africa, and probably also the jealousy of political rivals. Why does none of this appear in his poetry?

From the point of view of literary history, such questions are naive. A word or two about genre conventions or what was expected of poetry at the time would probably make them go away. But for the translator, with a communication gap to bridge, between languages and between centuries, simple questions can be useful and it is best not to bury them prematurely under technical information. One aspect of Garcilaso's poetry, however, may have to be taken on trust: the sound. Like Boscán, Garcilaso aimed to naturalize the smooth Italian forms in Spanish, and his success in doing so is confirmed by generations of readers and scholars who have delighted in the musicality of his verse. In poetry, sound trumps other arguments, but it is an element the translator cannot rest a case on. Translation by definition transfers the work into a language with a different sound system; whatever is put in its place may be justifiable but it cannot be the same. That aside, I hope that a closer look at the life and work may suggest answers (*suggest*, not give) to the simple questions. It was not simple to be Garcilaso and his poetry reflects more of his problems and is more directly relevant to his situation than the traditional account would lead us to believe.

Undoubtedly, Garcilaso made an important decision early in life, one which lifted him clear of a purely local destiny. He was among those who rendered homage when the new king, Charles V, first arrived in Valladolid at the end of 1517, and he remained in the king's service (later his viceroy's) until his death in action in 1536. Garcilaso was a second son, and to seek a position at court was an obvious choice, but it was not an automatic one.

Charles V's accession ended a long period of uncertainty that had lasted since the death of Isabel in 1505, a period in which even the union of Castile and Aragon had been threatened.[2] But Charles had never lived in Spain, did not speak Spanish, and brought with him a retinue of foreign advisers who filled the most lucrative posts, arousing great hostility, particularly in Castile. Many would have been reluctant to cooperate with a regime that appeared to be unfriendly to Spain's interests. To make matters worse, the new king, instead of visiting Toledo, went off to Zaragoza and Barcelona, which belonged to Aragon, not Castile. During this journey, Charles received news of his election as emperor on the death of his uncle Maximilian, and it became necessary for him to visit his new dominions. As Charles headed north to embark for Germany, Spain might have seemed destined for a period of inefficient rule by an absentee king. Before he left, the Cortes were summoned to Santiago in Galicia to vote the king a subsidy. The protests began even before he sailed and Garcilaso's elder brother, Pedro Laso, who represented their hometown of Toledo at the Cortes, was banished to Gibraltar for his part in the initial unrest.

With Charles gone, what became known as the rebellion of the *comuneros* started in earnest. Toledo was one of the most disaffected towns and there matters were complicated by the traditional rivalry of two powerful families, who lined up for and against the king. The royal administration was replaced by a commune headed by Pedro Laso and Juan de Padilla, who was later executed. When Pedro Laso's moderates were defeated by extremists in the rebel party, he fled to Portugal. Meanwhile Garcilaso and others loyal to the crown had been expelled from the town and for a time were besieged in the *castillo del Águila* just outside. Garcilaso, who around this time had been made a member of the king's special guard, was wounded at the battle of Olías when

2. After Isabel's death, Ferdinand was only regent in Castile.

the Toledo *comuneros* were defeated. On returning to Toledo, he found the house had been sacked. Considerable bitterness must have existed within the town between former neighbors and also, one would imagine, within Garcilaso's own family, but there was no permanent rift because he subsequently spent much time trying to obtain a pardon for his brother, who remained under threat of execution on Charles's return to Spain.

Fortunately, Garcilaso had chosen the winning side, the one that represented Spain's future. There were a number of reasons—beside financial gain—why he might have been attracted to it. Having Charles as king gave Spain a key political role in Europe and potentially an important cultural one as well. In addition to his unpopular foreign advisers, Charles brought to Spain the works of Erasmus, contributing to a heightened interest in humanism. His imperial title necessitated involvement with the rest of Europe, where his power was to become dominant, despite fierce competition from France. The Spanish possessions in Italy established Spanish power as chief defense against piracy and Turkish ambitions in the Mediterranean, and the first twenty years of the reign also brought a sudden expansion in the New World, with the adventures of Cortés in Mexico and Pizarro in Peru.

It is worth noting that Charles was about the same age as Garcilaso, who continued to prosper in the king's service, helped by the patronage of the house of Alba. He probably served in a successful campaign against the French in the Pyrenees and was present in 1525 when Charles first held his court in Toledo, having trumped the French king's pretensions by defeating and capturing him at Pavia and holding him hostage. It was probably at this time that Garcilaso met Boscán, and he could also have met people like Andrea Navagero, the Venetian ambassador; Baltasar Castiglione, author and Pope's ambassador; and Spanish writers like Diego López de Ayala, translator of Boccaccio and Sannazaro. An advantageous marriage was arranged for him by the king's sister, Leonor, to one of her ladies-in-waiting. Later he went with Charles to Italy and was present at the grand ceremony in Bologna where Charles was crowned as emperor by the Pope. When Leonor was married to the French king, he was sent on a diplomatic and spying mission to the French court (it seems there were suspicions about the treatment of Leonor). All went well until 1531, when family problems caught up with him.

At this point, we should probably consider the Isabel affair, which still crops up frequently in commentaries on Garcilaso's poetry. Isabel Freyre was a Portuguese gentlewoman in the service of Princess Isabel of Portugal. It is possible that Garcilaso met her on an earlier trip to Lisbon when he saw Pedro Laso, but the date usually suggested for his falling in love with her is 1526, when she accompanied the princess to Seville for her marriage to Charles V. This was about a year after Garcilaso's marriage to Elena de Zúñiga. Later, in 1528, Isabel married and in 1531 she died in childbirth. There is a note appended to Garcilaso's *Copla II* in one of the manuscripts that reads "Written for Isabel Freyre when she married a man who was beneath her in status" (see appendix A). Garcilaso never mentions her by name, but in the first eclogue one of his shepherd lovers complains of being abandoned for someone inferior and the other laments the death of the woman he loved in childbirth. Similar references can be found elsewhere in the poetry, and the spiritual presence, as it were, of Isabel has been used to distinguish and account for Garcilaso's best work. Where Isabel is concerned, the argument tends to be circular: his best poetry is superior because it expresses an emotion that is strong and sincere, and that can only be his love for Isabel, Isabel therefore inspired his best poetry; or else, since we know the poem is addressed to Isabel, the feelings expressed are sincere and therefore the poem must be good.

Not too long ago this romantic story received something of a blow from new information about Garcilaso's relations with the mother of his illegitimate son, Lorenzo. In his will, Garcilaso made provision for Lorenzo to be given a university education, but did not name his mother, who was later discovered to be

Guiomar Carrillo.[3] More recent research by María Carmen Vaquero has shown that Guiomar was from a good Toledo family and suggests that the relationship was more serious than had previously been thought. The family houses were in the same parish, so the two may have known each other from childhood. This set the scene for another romantic story of doomed love. Guiomar's family, like Garcilaso's elder brother, were probably on the wrong side in the *comunero* uprising. Suppose now Garcilaso had wanted to marry her and legitimize his son? As a servant of the emperor, he would certainly not have been allowed to. We can see the effect of unauthorized marriages from the event of 1531.

Garcilaso was in Ávila in 1531, preparing to depart for Germany to join the emperor's forces on a campaign against the Turks, when he was asked to witness the wedding of his nephew, Pedro Laso's son, also named Garcilaso, in the cathedral. The boy was fourteen and the bride, Isabel de la Cueva, eleven, so obviously this was not a romantic elopement but an arrangement favorable to family prestige and fortune. It appears to have been promoted by the girl's mother and maternal grandmother, distantly related to Garcilaso's family; the rest of the de la Cueva family were unhappy with it because the family name would be lost, the girl being heir to the family's head, the duke of Albuquerque. A letter from Carlos V in Brussels to the empress in Spain, dated September 4, 1531, enjoins her to prevent it. But arrangements for the wedding had been made in the spring and it went ahead without royal consent. Afterward, Garcilaso left with the Duke of Alba for Germany, but he was stopped in Tolosa and questioned, and when his answers were unsatisfactory he was banned from the court. When they caught up with the main army in Germany, despite the intercession of the Duke of Alba the emperor had him detained on an island in the Danube; he

---

3. A university education was not quite what it is nowadays, but would have prepared Lorenzo for a church position (not like his father as a courtier, or for a military career).

writes of this in Song III. This punishment ended quite soon, but the order banning him from court was not rescinded and he was sent to serve under Don Pedro de Toledo, the duke of Alba's uncle, who was the new viceroy of Naples.

Opinions differ as to how far the posting to Naples reflects the emperor's continued displeasure. There are cases where Garcilaso was refused advantages solicited for him by the powerful Alba family, suggesting that he was still in disgrace, and he never returned to live in Spain. However, it did not prevent his being used to carry important messages to the emperor in Spain, or his fighting with the emperor's forces in the capture of Tunis, which we learn of in Sonnet XXXV and in the second elegy. However it may be, the posting to Italy gave him a huge opportunity to develop his poetic talents and assimilate Renaissance culture in its most dynamic environment. In Naples, he met Italian and Spanish humanists and came into contact with the new, post-Petrarchan generation of Italian poets: Pietro Bembo, Sannazaro, Tansillo, and Bernardo Tasso. Most of his poetic output dates from this period.

Three of his works in particular seem to say rather more than the rest about Garcilaso's own thoughts and feelings: the two elegies and the epistle to Boscán. Indeed they are so different from his sonnets, songs, and eclogues that one is reminded of Coleridge's conversation poems, written nearly three centuries later. Two of them provoked an interesting comment from Blanco White, a Spanish liberal living in self-imposed exile in nineteenth-century England. Writing to congratulate J. H. Wiffen on his recent translation of Garcilaso, Blanco White says, "I cannot help regretting that you have extended your labors to all Garcilasso's poems. The second elegy and the Epistle to Boscan [sic] are so perfectly devoid of merit that they stand like a dark spot, a perfect eyesore in the book. They should not, I conceive be presented to the public without a kind of apology. I do not like either the *Flor de Gnido* half so much as I used in my youth. The first part of the 3d Eclogue is very beautiful and you have done it full justice."[4] Blanco White's animosity toward the second elegy and the epistle is surprising, but his disapproval also of the ode and implied slight to the last part of the third eclogue almost certainly align him with the romanticizers who want the best poetry to be that which describes the poet's supposed real-life love for Isabel Freyre.

Garcilaso's "Epístola a Boscán," derived from the epistles of Horace, is the first poem to be written in Spanish in unrhyming hendecasyllables. For me, this simple poem addressed to a friend does almost more than the more ambitious and metrically complex eclogues to confirm that Garcilaso's true vocation was literature. Its main declared topic is friendship, but the poem is also a demonstration of the act of writing and the art of composition. It begins with some remarks on the topic of writing to a friend. Garcilaso says he takes pleasure in telling his friend whatever he is thinking, so there is never any problem finding a subject. Nor is there any need to strive for an elaborate style: one of the advantages of friendship is that it allows you in writing to use a "relaxed and unpretentious carelessness." This carelessness, or *descuido*, recalls Castiglione's precept for courtiers that they should have *sprezzatura*, or nonchalance, in all they do, since Boscán had used the same word, *descuido*, to translate *sprezzatura* in his Spanish version, *El Cortesano*. Castiglione's idea is not that the courtier should actually do things carelessly but that he should make it appear that way. You may have to work or practice as hard as anyone else, but the effort should not show. And this is exactly what happens in this poem, which appears to be a series of random thoughts precisely because it is organized to give that impression.

After discussing the theory of how to write to a friend, Garcilaso now has to get on with it, and he makes the transition in a manner that is anything but random with "and so . . . I shall

---

4. Robert Johnson, "Letters of Blanco White to J. H. Wiffen and Samuel Rogers," *Neophilologus* (Amsterdam: Springer) 52 (1968): 142.

say, *as to the first . . .*" (my italics). The first of the two advantages of writing to a friend he mentions is the ease of finding a subject. So in order to begin he chooses the subject with which such a letter might be expected to begin, the journey and his own health—like a modern postcard saying "arrived safely." He does not say how far he has traveled, but promises this information for the end of the letter, where the address he is writing from will conventionally appear. The letter now becomes the journey, the journey the letter: he allows his thoughts to wander as he allows his horse to wander, and eventually he starts to consider the subject of friendship and "the one who taught us friendship's proper path." I believe this refers to a specific person and most editors tell us it was Aristotle. But although Garcilaso makes some show of analyzing friendship, presumably in the manner of Aristotle or whichever authority he is referring to, what he really wants to do is to explain something that happens to him when he thinks of Boscán, "something great and seemingly strange," "una gran cosa, al parecer estraña" ("Epistle to Boscán," line 34). This, he says, is the delight that results from the disinterested love he gives Boscán, unilaterally and not for his own profit, something that is quite real and not (as love is often said to be) a madness.

Having reached this peak of intimacy (and perhaps self-exposure), Garcilaso covers the possible embarrassment with humor. He is embarrassed and ashamed, he says, to have praised the roads of France in a previous letter, because now he thinks nothing in France worth praising. To say he is embarrassed and ashamed about this is such an exaggeration that we know he cannot mean it; if there is embarrassment, it stems from the previous comments on friendship and love. He follows up with another joke about a fat friend in Barcelona and he ends with his present address, announced with an elegantly indirect allusion to Petrarch's Laura that presupposes his and Boscán's common interest in literature. The composition is a poem masquerading as a casual letter and has proceeded in the very writerly fashion of pretending to think aloud.

There is some of the same artful carelessness in the second elegy. Once again it begins like a letter, quite lightheartedly, telling where he is and what is going on there. Then comes the confession of having accidentally slipped into writing satire when his intention is to write an elegy, and we are made aware of the writer's controlling hand. This is followed by an apparently careless reference to the writing of poetry ("the muses") as a source of pleasure and an escape from serious business. Then the thought of returning to Naples brings thoughts of the mistress he left there and his jealous suspicion that she will have betrayed him leads to generalizations about the torture of uncertainty and the thought that it is perhaps less than the pain of knowing what one fears is true. This is followed by complaints about his military service: although he has just participated in a great victory, he does not remind us of this and evidently finds nothing in it to boast of. All he does is revert to the subject of jealousy and compare himself to a dying man who continues to hope for life because his wife cannot bear to tell him the worst. Such a man, in Christian homiletics, goes to hell because he dies unprepared, without repenting of his sins. Garcilaso says he too deceives himself with hopes he knows to be false, and this is no better than a form of suicide. These self-pitying thoughts are broken into abruptly by a vision of his friend, Boscán, at home, surrounded by those who love him, lulled by the sound of waves on the beautiful seashore, gazing at the woman he loves and who inspires his poetry. By contrast, Garcilaso sees himself as a "driven mercenary"; looking into the future he can see no escape, no relief except death, and he ends with one of his gloomiest lines: "así diverso entre contrarios muero," "thus divided between contraries I die" (line 193). So much for sprezzatura and the ideal of the carelessly versatile courtier! But the poem has demonstrated some of Garcilaso's typical skills: his ability to convey changing moods and to create contrasting images.

Gloomy pronouncements are frequent in Garcilaso's poetry, but it is often not easy to say what specifically gives rise to them.

The problem is that Garcilaso cultivates a kind of vagueness in relation to his feelings and his religious or philosophical views. In Song III, for example, he tells us that "a single hour undid / the long years of work / to gain what my whole life passed in pursuit of" (lines 43–45); or, more literally, "in a single hour / all *that* has been undone / *on which* I spent my whole life" (my italics). However you translate it, there is no clear referent for "all that ... on which ..." We do not know what he has spent his whole life on, what has been undone. We only know for sure that it is something that makes his need very pressing ("que es mi necesidad muy apretada," line 42) and that as a result nothing else now can scare him. Given the context, we assume that it has something to do with love, just as in the preceding stanza we assume that "something else, harder than death" (line 37), refers to unhappy love. Yet the knowing, allusive tone draws us on to look for more and in the "undone" we may seem to glimpse a whole life unraveling.

A similar ambivalence in Garcilaso's poetry stems from his deliberate use of a language that will apply equally to Christian and classical worldviews. Notably in the first elegy, many expressions support either a stoic or a Christian account of life and death. The current situation, in which Don Fernando and his family mourn the death of Fernando's younger brother, is placed in a classical landscape. Fernando is compared to the sister of Phaeton, mourning her brother, burnt to death when he was allowed to drive the chariot of his father, the sun god Apollo; the mother and sisters are accompanied in their grieving by the river Tormes, portrayed as an old man leaning on an urn, and by nymphs and satyrs and suchlike classical paraphernalia. As models for Fernando's need to overcome his grief, Garcilaso cites the Trojans calling a halt to their tears after the death of Hector, and Venus "moving on" after the death of Adonis. In view of your position, he says to Don Fernando, it is your duty to meet adversity "with resolute countenance and valiant heart" ("con firme rostro y corazón valiente," line 189), for this is the hard road that must be traveled to reach "the high throne of immortality; one who strays will not arrive there" ("de la inmortalidad el alto asiento, / do nunca arriba quien d'aquí declina," lines 202–4). The difficult path of virtue is a concept that fits either Christian doctrine or classical ethics. In Garcilaso's fusion of the two, only the goal presents a slight problem. "The high throne of immortality" is clearly the temple of fame, rather than Christian heaven. But a little later he advises Don Fernando to turn his eyes to the quarter "where the supreme hope beckons" ("donde al fin te llama / la suprema esperanza," line 250), to which the soul ascends perfected and purged in a pure flame. This certainly sounds like purgatory and heaven, but as if to forestall too narrow an interpretation, Garcilaso suggests the flame is identical to the pyre of Hercules, when the hero's spirit flew up to "the high goal" ("la alta meta," line 255). Thus he equates the classical and Christian accounts of the afterlife. Later, he assures Don Fernando that his brother, by climbing the difficult high path, has reached "the sweet region of joy" ("la dulce región del alegría," line 261), which is clearly heaven, whether in a classical or a Christian mode. Such ambivalence is, of course, a general feature of Renaissance poetry, but in Garcilaso it contributes to the uncertainty, the mixture of resolution and skepticism, which is part of his poetic persona.

The dark language of despair, so typical of Garcilaso's poetry, is also nonspecific. Love and the lover's jealousy may be a starting point, as in Sonnets XXX and XXXII, or the second elegy, but Garcilaso's real topic is not love but loss, a universal experience and one that does not demand any single biographical explanation. When in the first eclogue Nemoroso contemplates a world without Elisa, he expresses his total disorientation:

> a tide of darkness
> rises to shroud the earth in black and brings

terrors of the night that freeze our senses,
and the horrifying forms that things assume.
when night conceals their usual shape from us . . .

::::

    se levanta
la negra escuridad que'l mundo cubre,
de do viene el temor que nos espanta
y la medrosa forma en que s'ofrece
aquella, que la noche nos encubre . . .

In the celebrated Sonnet X, "O sweet mementoes, unfortunately found" ("Oh dulces prendas, por mi mal halladas"), a series of contrasting terms expresses the difference between the happy past and present misery, justifying the speaker's linking of memory and death (words that in Spanish are strongly alliterative). But while happiness accumulates over time, loss is immediate:

Since in one moment you took it all away,
the happiness you'd given over time.

::::

Pues en una hora junto me llevastes
todo el bien que por términos me distes.
(lines 9–10)

The carpe diem theme is always ambivalent, like a half-full, half-empty glass, but in Sonnet XXIII the emphasis is less on seizing the moment than on the inevitability of change and the loss of youth and beauty. Sonnet XXV laments that fate "with destroying hands" ("con manos dañosas") has felled the tree and scattered the fruit and flowers, leaving the speaker with nothing to do but weep over the grave, "until by the dark of that eternal night / these eyes of mine that saw you shall be closed" ("hasta que aquella eterna noche escura / me cierre aquestos ojos que te vieron," lines 12–13). Although the sonnet does not end here but concludes with "leaving me with other eyes to see you" ("deján-dome con otros que te vean," line 14), it does not sound much like a message of hope. Sonnet XXXII finds him entirely deprived of hope, though here, ostensibly, the sonnet deals with a pilgrim-age of love and there is no explicit reference to literal death:

And most of all what I lack now's the light
of hope, that used to guide me as I strayed
through the dark and lonely land of your disdain.
:::
sobre todo, me falta ya la lumbre
de la esperanza, con que andar solía
por la oscura región de vuestro olvido.

(lines 12–14)

That "used to" ("andar solía") is typical: what used to be is al-ways better than what is now; everything good is now lacking or lost.

But loss is not absolute if it can be compensated. The stories depicted in the third eclogue—Orpheus and Eurydice, Apollo and Daphne, Venus and Adonis, and the dead nymph Elisa—are stories about loss, but in each one loss is transmuted into art. This is realized within the fiction, because each story is depicted in a beautiful tapestry one of the nymphs is making; it is en-hanced by the association with the art of Greece and Rome; and, above all, it is owing to the power of Garcilaso's verse. Art may be invoked even in less benign circumstances: the nymphs in Sonnet XI belong to a beautiful underwater dreamworld, even if for the speaker to join them implies drowning. In the first elegy, mourning is relieved by a vision of Venus that makes the whole world rejoice (lines 223–40); art generates the energy that can dispel the gloom. Both Eclogues I and III, which are the culmi-nation of Garcilaso's poetry, present idealized pastoral worlds in which suffering has been transmuted into art and at each poem's ending tranquility prevails.

Though Eclogues I and III have virtually no action, they move with the emotion that drives them, their changing moods. In the first, for example, Salicio's "song" of jealousy fluctuates between pain, indignation, and regret and ends in self-pitying resignation. The idyllic opening of Nemoroso's "song" concentrates on the happy time and his unawareness *then* of the pain he feels *now*. After the terrors of the night, to which Elisa's death condemns him, the nightingale's song conveys the message that suffering may be turned into beauty. A lock of Elisa's hair brings momentary relief, but this is immediately followed by the tormenting vision of her on her deathbed. The penultimate stanza contemplates a future in which the "veil of the body" is broken and they will wander hand in hand among other mountains, rivers, and valleys, and he will have no further fear of losing her. The last stanza announces the peaceful end of day and the two shepherds return home "as if / awakening from a dream" ("recordando / ambos como de sueño," lines 17–18). This ending distances the poem from reality, emphasizing the work of imagination.

Eclogue III is emotionally even more distanced. The sad stories are represented in tapestries, not as experiences of the speaker. The two shepherds' paired songs at the end, a device borrowed from Virgil, cannot possibly be taken as an expression of the poet's real-life feelings for anyone, which possibly explains why Blanco White endorsed only the first part of this eclogue. The opening, with its articulate flattery, elegant hyperbole, and gentle humor, suggests a writer secure in his powers and confident that he is loved and appreciated by his peers (as indeed he was, according to what we know of Garcilaso's intimacy with humanist and literary circles in Naples). The tone is reminiscent of the kind of subtle, open-minded conversation Castiglione records in his book. The setting for what follows could be an idealization of real childhood memories of the river outside Toledo: a hidden paradise on the banks of the Tagus, to which nymphs of the classical world might well return. Both this and the view of Toledo depicted in the fourth nymph's tapestry are described with enthusiasm and there is no reason to doubt Garcilaso's sincerity in commending the countryside bathed by the river's waters as "the happiest region of the whole of Spain" (line 200).

Garcilaso's melancholy is a distinctive quality of his poetry, but it cannot be attributed to a single fulminating passion. The sense of loss can be aroused by contemplation of many things besides a lover's betrayal: time, change, failure, death, even the withdrawal of favor by a friend, an employer, or Fate. The references in Eclogue I that fit the case of Isabel Freyre, the marriage to someone considered inferior, the death in childbirth, only establish that Garcilaso could have had her in mind, but do not prove that Salicio or Nemoroso speak directly for him. On the contrary, the self-pitying tone of Salicio's complaints is a little too much like examples in *The Book of the Courtier*, which show that a lover's overinsistence is more likely to alienate the woman than gain her sympathy. Castiglione, in fact, provides an antidote to tears in the good humor and wit with which his assembly of male and female aristocrats and intellectuals discuss the psychology of love toward the end of that book, a book which we know Garcilaso had read. In Eclogue III, the dead nymph of Nise's tapestry, whose name is to be carried down to the Lusitanian sea, may in some sense be inspired by Isabel Freyre. But we should note that the indirection is extreme, a recession from an imagined "real" situation, in which the poet is addressing his patron, the "illustrious and most beautiful Maria," deep into the imaginary world of art: the supposed words of the dead nymph tell how her name, Elisa, uttered by Nemoroso in his grief, is picked up and carried to Portugal by the river Tagus, but these words are in fact imagined by one of the goddesses mourning Elisa's death who is carving them on a tree; and this goddess is portrayed in Nise's tapestry, and Nise is one of the four nymphs in the story the poet has offered to tell his patron.

There is no doubt that Garcilaso's choice of the pastoral is deliberate. He makes it clear in Song V that he has no intention of writing an epic: if like Orpheus he could control the world with his poetry, he would not sing of "angry Mars / dedicated to death, / his countenance stained with powder, blood and sweat" (lines 13–15), but only of the power of beauty. In the dedicatory stanzas of the first eclogue, Garcilaso excuses himself for not recording the viceroy in his martial or hunting role and begs a hearing for his shepherds until he has time to write something more suitable. Instead of the laurel of victory, he says, let it be the turn of the ivy. Ivy represents the pastoral as well as the humility of the poet, climbing in the shadow of his patron's fame. Apart from the last section of the second eclogue (not included here), which proclaims the military exploits of the Albas, Garcilaso shows no inclination for the epic. Elsewhere in the poetry, Mars is "bloodthirsty Mars" (Eclogue III, line 37) "cruel, fearsome and relentless Mars" (Elegy II, line 94), and is generally associated with the word *furor*, fury or madness. There is an extended expression of antiwar sentiment in Elegy I (lines 82–92):

Which of us now's not hurt by the excess
of wars, of danger and of banishment?
Who is not weary of the endless process?
    Who has not seen his blood spill on the blade
of his enemy? Who has not thought to die
a thousand times, and escaped by accident?
    How many have lost, will lose, their wife, their house
and their good name and how many others
will see their fortune plundered or dispersed?
    And for all this, what do we get? A little
glory? A prize, a word of gratitude?
:::
    ¿A quién ya de nosotros el eceso
de guerras, de peligros y destierro
no toca, y no ha cansado el gran proceso?
    ¿Quién no vio desparcir su sangre al hierro
del enemigo? ¿Quién no vio su vida

perder mil veces y escapar por yerro?
¡De cuantos queda y quedará perdida
la casa, la mujer y la memoria,
y d'otros la hacienda desperdida!
¿Qué se saca d'aquesto? ¿Alguna gloria?
¿Algunos premios o agradecimiento?

And as Richard Helgerson points out, the sonnet from *La Goleta* (Sonnet XXXV) moves away from the idea of military conquest with which it begins to end in identification with the tragic fate of Dido, putting individual suffering and the destruction of Tunis or Carthage in the balance against imperial ambition.

What Garcilaso explicitly complains about, however, is not warfare but the duties that leave him too little time for poetry. The famous line about taking up "now the pen and now the sword" in the fifth stanza of the third eclogue has often been taken as evidence that Garcilaso was the perfect Renaissance man, turning effortlessly from one activity to the other. The modern statue erected to him in a small square of his native Toledo near where the family house once stood shows him in a heroic posture brandishing a quill in one hand, with the other resting on the pommel of his sword. Yet the words in the poem can just as well be taken as a complaint about how difficult it is to maintain the balance. In the second elegy, Garcilaso tells us that he sustains himself on diversity, but "not without difficulty" (line 30), though he assures us he has no intention of giving up the muses. Garcilaso's sense of being divided and at war with himself must surely be related to his being pulled in different directions. In a sense, like the metamorphosis of Daphne into a tree, which becomes both cause and effect of Apollo's tears, poetry for Garcilaso was both problem and solution. It made demands on his time, but offered the only chance of redeeming time.

Probably one reason why Garcilaso does not write about war is that it was part of what he calls work, or "business" ("negocios"), and he wanted his poetry to be different, separate from that part of his life. When Garcilaso presents himself in a poem, he is holding the pen, not the sword, and in the second elegy, written just after a famous victory in which he was wounded, he speaks not of the action but of the rewards people expect to get from it. Yet although he does not beat the imperial drum, there is no suggestion that Garcilaso would have dismissed the concept of duty or disowned the military enterprises of Charles V. His attitude might be compared to the British war poets of World War I: Wilfred Owen abhorred the suffering and waste of life in the trenches but remained strongly loyal to those he fought alongside. Siegfried Sassoon, who made a serious protest against the war, was brave in battle to the point of recklessness. So too was Garcilaso, if we believe the story of his death, which has him leading an advance patrol to capture a tower in which some peasants were holding up the army's progress. He was first up the ladder and they dropped a stone on him, knocking him off and fatally injuring him. If he did not write of war it was not for lack of military experience or valor, or lack of ambition, but because pastoral or lyric poetry was in tune with his temperament, alert to the vagaries of human psychology and the more subtle power of language.[5]

Still more important is the fact that the making of verse in the Italian mode was in itself a serious affair. We should not be fooled by the apparent nonchalance with which Boscán and Garcilaso sometimes refer to poetry. To both men, the new poetry was not an escape into unreality but an enterprise involving

5. Sir Thomas Wyatt, a contemporary of Garcilaso's, had similar experiences, but they affected his poetry quite differently. Spenser, though much later, makes a more interesting comparison. In Garcilaso's case, however, we have no evidence of literature and political ambition mingling as they did at Elizabeth's court, according to Stephen Greenblatt's account in chapter four of Renaissance Self-Fashioning (Chicago: University of Chicago Press, 1980; rev. 2005). Charles V does not seem to have been particularly interested in poetry or to have been aware of Garcilaso's budding reputation as a poet. Similarly, Garcilaso himself never addressed the emperor in his poetry or sought to influence him by literary means (if one excludes the rather defiant complaint at his punishment in the third song, which would surely have been counterproductive in any case).

national pride. Spain, like Italy, could emulate the cultural glories of ancient Greece and Rome. Such a vision had inspired the *Gramática Castellana* of Antonio de Nebrija published in 1492 (that grandly significant date in Spanish history), the first grammar of a modern Romance language. It was as much political as cultural and affected even Charles V, who delighted in playing the part of Caesar. Culturally, there was a line from Petrarch to Dante and the Provençal poets, including the Valencian, Ausías March, and reaching back to Rome and, before that, to Greece, as Boscán spells out in a letter to the duchess of Soma that he used as preface to the second book of his and Garcilaso's poetry. The same tradition unfolds in England, with Wyatt and Surrey, Spenser and Sidney, as well as continuing later in Spain through Lope de Vega and Luis de Góngora, and the other poets of the Golden Age.

It is important to grasp the nature of this enterprise and its seriousness, because it helps us also to understand the continual imitation and borrowing that goes on among the poets of this period. This was not reprehensible plagiarism; quite the reverse, in fact. To borrow as Garcilaso does from Virgil and Horace, from Ovid, Petrarch, Sannazaro, and Tasso, or from Ausías March, was proof of modernity, of being up-to-date with the latest trends, at home in the contemporary language of the arts. It was thus that Garcilaso formed the language that enabled Spanish literature to achieve its most glorious manifestation in the golden age, at just the moment when the political drive was beginning to falter. His success can be measured by the continual echoes of his poetry in Spanish literature and by the fact that his name and influence have long outlived the empire. References to Garcilaso's poetry and even whole lines of his verse crop up everywhere. To some contemporaries, like Cristóbal de Castillejo, Garcilaso and Boscán produced something that sounded like gibberish, but not long after their deaths it had become the characteristic poetic sound of the Spanish Renaissance. When the eponymous glass graduate of Cervantes's story sets out on his travels, he takes only two of his many books: a devotional work and "a Garcilaso without commentary." There is scarcely a page of Góngora that does not contain some borrowing from Garcilaso; in two different sonnets he uses verbatim a line from the opening of Garcilaso's third eclogue, "Illustrious and most beautiful Maria." Clearly this is not because Góngora needs to enhance his own work by purloining some striking image, but because it was natural to demonstrate his familiarity with the founder of modern Spanish poetic style.

Finally, despite its pastoral themes, Garcilaso's poetry cannot be viewed as an escape from the harsher side of life. Death is always present. Ignacio Navarrete has drawn attention to the increasing violence and sexuality in the four tapestries of the third eclogue, generally considered Garcilaso's masterpiece. Certainly the stories themselves are at odds with the innocent beauty of the setting: Orpheus and Eurydice, a tale of longing and despair; Daphne and Apollo, a picture of frustrated desire; Venus and Adonis, full of blood and bereavement; and, finally, the dead nymph—undoubtedly dead, even if it is not clear how and why. There is controversy as to whether or not Garcilaso actually wrote "degollada" to describe her, and if he did, what it might mean. But whether we take its most literal sense, "with her throat cut," or see her as simply lying dead in the grass, she must represent the destruction of beauty and innocence. In this poem, there is as great a division between contraries as within the poet himself, and there can be no release into tranquility until the dreadful pictures have been painted and the two shepherds have sung their songs relating love's joy and pain to nature. Garcilaso refers to the story of Orpheus and Eurydice again in one of his sonnets (XV, not included here), in which he claims that he is more deserving of sympathy than Orpheus, because what he mourns is the loss of himself, not of something external to himself (as Eurydice is to Orpheus). On the face of it, this is a rather selfish and ungallant view, but if we relate it to the poetry as a whole, it may be illuminating. Garcilaso's concern is not a personal love affair with some unattainable lady, real or symbolic, but a search for identity. And what his poetry expresses is a sense of life as a continuing encounter with loss, an ill for which art is the only cure.

The problems of translating Garcilaso do not arise from complications of vocabulary or syntax. What is challenging is the very simplicity of his style, its apparent ease and directness. The primary concern must be to convey something of the music of his verse, which has been admired in all ages and is agreed to be his important contribution to Spanish literature. Unfortunately, nowadays this carries the risk of making him sound old-fashioned, when to his contemporaries he was startlingly modern. It is not helped either by the fact that his epithets are mainly conventional: grass is green and swans are white, water is pure and crystalline and pleasure sweet. Modern taste likes more surprises and spikier rhythms. To Garcilaso's contemporaries, on the other hand, it was exactly the smoothness that made his poetry sound so right in Spanish, despite its Italian roots. At the level of interpretation, there is also a problem of balance: one wants to preserve the underlying mystery of his poetry, its suggestive ambivalence, without giving an impression of uncertainty or fuzziness, which would belie Garcilaso's mastery of the medium.

I owe very special thanks to my generous helpers: Maria-Elena Pickett for her advice on meanings (and for memorably describing Garcilaso as "slippery" when I was struggling with his difficult simplicity); Simon Ellis for his close attention to the poetry; and likewise Martin Murphy, who also drew my attention to Blanco White's views on Wiffen's nineteenth-century translation. I am also especially grateful to Randolph Petilos of the University of Chicago Press who initiated the project, and to the Press's two anonymous readers who gave me great encouragement and valuable advice.

I must also record a serious debt to Richard Helgerson's *A Sonnet from Carthage*, which reached me not long after I had decided various difficulties in Garcilaso's second elegy were something I must attempt to unravel if I were to proceed. Here and there, my translations may differ from his, but the general direction of his book gave me invaluable help.

The text is taken from T. Navarro Tomás, without the accents that are not used in modern Spanish. There are also a few changes that affect meaning and these are pointed out in the notes.

Chronology

Anonymous portrait assumed to be Garcilaso de la Vega (sixteenth century).

Sonnets

There are around forty sonnets, give or take a few of doubtful authenticity. There is a slight variation in the numbering of them in different editions, but so far as I know there is not an edition that reflects a supposed order of composition, so I have simply followed the numbering in the 1911 edition of Navarro Tomás, which was to hand. A few can be dated from their relation to events. Otherwise style is the clue to differentiate between earlier poems, which show the influence of traditional Spanish poetry, and those that are more mature and more completely Italianate. But considering Garcilaso's life was short, his writing career even shorter, and his output small and not especially varied, the question of dating seems less important than it might with a more prolific poet. His best poetry was written in a period of about four years, between 1532, when he was banished from the Spanish court, and his death in 1536.

A comparison with his two *coplas* in appendix A can indicate what the Renaissance sonnet form gave Garcilaso: the sense of a forward movement, of an unfolding argument that culminates in a neat conclusion, building on what went before rather than just repeating it. His coplas seem to achieve unity only by shuffling a limited pack of words, rather than developing ideas, and give us more the sense of a game than an expression of thought or emotion. Of course the effect of the sonnets is greatly assisted by the hendecasyllable, the longer line which when well used is flowing and musical and much better adapted to conveying mood or emotion.

I have included Sonnet X and Sonnet XXIII, which often appear in anthologies as examples of Garcilaso's most accomplished poetry. The rest I selected either because I found some particular interest in them or because I felt the translation remained reasonably close to the original in sound and sense. Other sonnets known or thought to be from the later period are Sonnets XI, XIII, XXV, XXX, XXXIII, and XXXV. As far as I could manage I have followed the rhyme scheme of the original.

Soneto I

Cuando me paro a contemplar mi estado,
y a ver los pasos por do me han traído,
hallo, según por do anduve perdido,
que a mayor mal pudiera haber llegado;

mas cuando del camino estó olvidado,   5
a tanto mal no sé por dó he venido;
sé que me acabo, y más he yo sentido
ver acabar comigo mi cuidado.

Yo acabaré, que me entregué sin arte
a quien sabrá perderme y acabarme,   10
si ella quisiere, y aun sabrá querello;

que pues mi voluntad puede matarme,
la suya, que no es tanto de mi parte,
pudiendo, ¿qué hará sino hacello?

Sonnet I

When I stop to view my situation
and contemplate the steps that brought me here,
seeing the dangers of the way, I feel
I might have reached a far worse destination;

but when I cease to think about the journey,   5
I wonder that my state should be so bad;
I know I'm finished, and what most makes me sad
is thinking how this love of mine ends with me.

I'm finished, through my innocent surrender
to one able to end me, able to kill   10
if so she wishes . . . and able too to wish it;

for if I can be killed by my own will,
then her will, so much less in my favor,
being able, what will it do but do it?

Soneto V

Escrito está en mi alma vuestro gesto,
y cuanto yo escrebir de vos deseo;
vos sola lo escrebistes, yo lo leo
tan solo, que aun de vos me guardo en esto.

En esto estoy y estaré siempre puesto;   5
que aunque no cabe en mí cuanto en vos veo,
de tanto bien lo que no entiendo creo,
tomando ya la fe por presupuesto.

Yo no nací sino para quereros;
mi alma os ha cortado a su medida;   10
por hábito del alma misma os quiero.

Cuanto tengo confieso yo deberos;
por vos nací, por vos tengo la vida,
por vos he de morir y por vos muero.

Sonnet V

Your countenance is written in my soul,
and everything I'd wish to write about you;
you wrote it there yourself, while all I do
is read—still with an attitude that's fearful.

This is, and will always be, my occupation;   5
and though for all I see my soul lacks space,
I still believe in a good beyond my grasp,
given that faith's the primary assumption.

I was only born so I could love you:
my soul has cut you to its own dimensions,   10
as my soul's own habit I must have you;

everything I have I know I owe you;
for you was I born, for you I hold my life;
for you I will die, am dying, here and now.

Soneto X

¡Oh dulces prendas, por mi mal halladas,
dulces y alegres cuando Dios quería!
Juntas estáis en la memoria mía,
y con ella en mi muerte conjuradas.

¿Quién me dijera, cuando en las pasadas   5
horas en tanto bien por vos me vía,
que me habíades de ser en algún día
con tan grave dolor representadas?

Pues en un hora junto me llevastes
todo el bien que por términos me distes,   10
llevadme junto el mal que me dejastes.

Si no, sospecharé que me pusistes
en tantos bienes, porque deseastes
verme morir entre memorias tristes.

Sonnet X

O sweet mementoes, unfortunately found,
sweet and also, when God willed it, happy!
You live together in my memory
and, with memory conspiring, plot my end.

When in those times, now forever fled,   5
your presence was such happiness to me,
how could I imagine you would be
with such a pain as this revisited?

Since in one moment you took it all away,
the happiness you'd given over time,   10
take away too this pain that you have left me;

or else I shall suppose you only showed me
such happiness because it was your aim
among sad memories to see me die.

Soneto XI

Hermosas ninfas, que en el río metidas,
contentas habitáis en las moradas
de relucientes piedras fabricadas
y en colunas de vidrio sostenidas;

agora estéis labrando embebecidas,   5
o tejiendo las telas delicadas;
agora unas con otras apartadas,
contándoos los amores y las vidas;

dejad un rato la labor, alzando
vuestras rubias cabezas a mirarme,   10
y no os dentendréis mucho según ando;

que o no podréis de lástima escucharme,
o convertido en agua aquí llorando,
podréis allá de espacio consolarme.

Sonnet XI

Slender nymphs who dwell within the river,
contentedly inhabiting those halls
that are constructed out of shining jewels
and underset by colonnades of crystal,

whether bowed over your embroidery,   5
or toiling at the weaver's delicate art,
or whether sitting in little groups apart
making your loves and lives into a story,

for a moment set aside what you are doing
and raise your lovely heads to view my plight;   10
you won't spend long, for such is my present state

either for pity you will shrink from listening
or, when weeping turns me into water here,
there'll be time enough to comfort me down there.

Soneto XIII

A Dafne ya los brazos le crecían,
y en luengos ramos vueltos se mostraban;
en verdes hojas vi que se tornaban
los cabellos que al oro escurecían.

De áspera corteza se cubrían   5
los tiernos miembros, que aún bullendo estaban;
los blancos pies en tierra se hincaban,
y en torcidas raíces se volvían.

Aquel que fué la causa de tal daño,
a fuerza de llorar, crecer hacía   10
este árbol que con lágrimas regaba.

¡Oh miserable estado, oh mal tamaño!
¡Que con lloralla cresca cada día
la causa y la razón por que lloraba!

Sonnet XIII

Daphne's arms were growing: now they were seen
taking on the appearance of slim branches;
those tresses, which discountenanced gold's brightness,
were, as I watched, turning to leaves of green;

the delicate limbs still quivering with life   5
became scarfed over with a rough skin of bark,
the white feet to the ground were firmly stuck,
changed into twisted roots, which gripped the earth.

He who was the cause of this great evil
so wildly wept the tree began to grow,   10
because with his tears he watered it himself.

O wretched state, o monumental ill,
that the tears he weeps should cause each day to grow
that which is cause and motive for his grief.

Soneto XVII

Pensando que el camino iba derecho,
vine a parar en tanta desventura,
que imaginar no puedo, aun con locura,
algo de que esté un rato satisfecho.

El ancho campo me parece estrecho;   5
la noche clara para mí es escura;
la dulce compañía, amarga y dura,
y duro campo de batalla el lecho.

Del sueño, si hay alguno, aquella parte
sola que es ser imagen de la muerte   10
se aviene con el alma fatigada.

En fin, que como quiera, estoy de arte,
que juzgo ya por hora menos fuerte,
aunque en ella me vi, la que es pasada.

Sonnet XVII

Thinking that the road I took was straight,
I landed in such misery it seems
that now I cannot conceive, in wildest dreams,
anything that would content me for a moment.

The open countryside's a narrow cage,   5
the beauty of moonlight is dark night to me,
while hard and bitter is sweet company
and my bed hard as the ground where battles rage;

of sleep, if it comes, I welcome only the part
that is an aspect of death's gloomy image,   10
for that alone accords with my weary soul.

And, say what you will, I'm now in such a state
I hold this present pain to be more savage
than anything in the past, though its pain was real.

Soneto XXIII

En tanto que de rosa y azucena
se muestra la color en vuestro gesto,
y que vuestro mirar ardiente, honesto,
con clara luz la tempestad serena;

y en tanto que el cabello, que en la vena   5
del oro se escogió, con vuelo presto,
por el hermoso cuello blanco, enhiesto,
el viento mueve, esparce y desordena;

coged de vuestra alegre primavera
el dulce fruto, antes que el tiempo airado   10
cubra de nieve la hermosa cumbre,

Marchitará la rosa el viento helado,
todo lo mudará la edad ligera,
por no hacer mudanza en su costumbre.

Sonnet XXIII

While colors of the lily and the rose
are displayed within the outline of your face,
and with that look, both passionate and chaste,
storms grow still in the clear light of your eyes;

and while your hair that seems to have been mined   5
from seams of gold, and seeming too in flight
about that neck, so white, so bravely upright,
is moved and spread and scattered by the wind,

seize the sweet fruits of your joyous spring,
now, before angry time creates a waste,   10
summoning snow to hide the glorious summit:

the rose will wither in the icy blast
and fickle time will alter everything,
if only to be constant in its habit.

Soneto XXV

¡Oh hado esecutivo en mis dolores,
cómo sentí tus leyes rigurosas!
Cortaste el árbol con manos dañosas,
y esparciste por tierra fruta y flores.

En poco espacio yacen mis amores   5
y toda la esperanza de mis cosas,
tornadas en cenizas desdeñosas,
y sordas a mis quejas y clamores.

Las lágrimas que en esta sepultura
se vierten hoy en día y se vertieron   10
recibe, aunque sin fruto allá te sean,

hasta que aquella eterna noche escura
me cierre aquestos ojos que te vieron,
dejándome con otros que te vean.

Sonnet XXV

O fate, so active to promote my troubles,
how hard I find your laws have been to me;
with your destroying hands you felled the tree
and scattered on the ground the fruits and flowers.

In a narrow space my unbounded love now lies   5
together with all the hopes I ever had;
all are turned to ashes, disdainful, cold
and deaf to my complaints and to my cries.

Accept the tears that on this grave are spilt
today, and those that in the past you caused,   10
albeit there they have no value to you,

until by the dark of that eternal night
these eyes of mine that saw you shall be closed,
leaving me with other eyes to see you.

Soneto XXX

Sospechas, que en mi triste fantasía
puestas, hacéis la guerra a mi sentido,
volviendo y revolviendo el afligido
pecho, con dura mano, noche y día;

ya se acabó la resistencia mía   5
y la fuerza del alma; ya rendido
vencer de vos me dejo, arrepentido
de haberos contrastado en tal porfía.

Llevadme a aquel lugar tan espantable,
do por no ver mi muerte allí esculpida,   10
cerrados hasta aquí tuve los ojos.

Las armas pongo ya; que concedida
no es tan larga defensa al miserable;
colgad en vuestro carro mis despojos.

Sonnet XXX

Suspicion, how you occupy my sad
imagination and on my senses prey
when with rough hands you are busy night and day,
poking and probing inside my ruined head;

it's done, I'm finished, my opposition's ended,   5
you win, I have no further will to fight,
I surrender to you and what's more regret
that in the past so bitterly I contended.

Lead me, then, to the place where fear prevails:
until now, I shut my eyes and would not see,   10
not daring to confront my imaged death;

I lay my arms aside, to a wretch like me
it's not given to resist you at such length;
now on your chariot you may hang the spoils.

Soneto XXXII

Estoy contino en lágrimas bañado,
rompiendo el aire siempre con sospiros;
y más me duele nunca osar deciros
que he llegado por vos a tal estado,

que viéndome do estoy y en lo que he andado   5
por el camino estrecho de seguiros,
si me quiero tornar para huiros,
desmayo viendo atrás lo que he dejado;

si a subir pruebo, en la difícil cumbre,
a cada paso espántanme en la vía   10
ejemplos tristes de los que han caído.

Y sobre todo, fáltame la lumbre
de la esperanza, con que andar solía
por la escura región de vuestro olvido.

Sonnet XXXII

I am continually half drowned in tears,
my sighs mounting to heaven every day,
and what most hurts me is I dare not say
that, of this state I'm in, you are the cause;

and when I see what distance I have done   5
along the narrow road I tread to serve you,
and think how I might turn around and leave you,
I tremble, seeing all that must be foregone;

but climbing on toward the distant summit,
at every step I take I am dismayed   10
by the grim example of all those who've fallen.

And most of all what I lack now's the light
of hope, that used to guide me as I strayed
through the dark and lonely land of your disdain.

Soneto XXXIII

Mario, el ingrato amor, como testigo
de mi fe pura y de mi gran firmeza,
usando en mí su vil naturaleza,
que es hacer más ofensa al más amigo;

teniendo miedo que si escribo o digo   5
su condición, abajo su grandeza,
no bastando su fuerza a su crueza,
ha esforzado la mano a su enemigo.

Y así, en la parte que la diestra mano
gobierna, y en aquella que declara   10
los concetos del alma, fuí herido.

Mas yo haré que aquesta ofensa, cara
le cueste al ofensor, que ya estoy sano,
libre, desesperado y ofendido.

Sonnet XXXIII
To Mario at a time when according to some the poet was wounded in
the tongue and the arm

Mario, Love the ingrate having observed
the purity of my faith, my constancy,
resolved to use on me the baseness he
reserves for those by whom he best is served;

and fearing to lose face if men understand   5
his true nature from what I write or say,
yet lacking strength of his own to satisfy
his cruelty, he annexed my enemy's hand;

and so, in the part which manages my right
hand and in that which clothes in speaking sense   10
the concepts of the soul, I have been wounded.

But I will make sure this cowardly offence
costs the offender dear, for now I'm fit
and free and desperate and offended.

Soneto XXXV
A Boscán desde La Goleta

Boscán, las armas y el furor de Marte,
que con su propia sangre el africano
suelo regando, hacen que el romano
imperio reverdesca en esta parte,

han reducido a la memoria el arte   5
y el antiguo valor italiano,
por cuya fuerza y valerosa mano
Africa se aterró de parte a parte.

Aquí donde el romano encendimiento,
donde el fuego y la llama licenciosa   10
sólo el nombre dejaron a Cartago,

vuelve y revuelve amor mi pensamiento,
hiere y enciende el alma temerosa,
y en llanto y en ceniza me deshago.

Sonnet XXXV
To Boscán from La Goleta

Arms, Boscán, and the fury of rampant Mars,
that, cultivating with their modern power
the soil of Africa, persuade the empire
of Rome to burgeon in these parts once more,

have reawakened, brought again to mind,   5
Italy's art, Italy's ancient valor
by means of which, with gallant deeds and power,
Africa was laid low from end to end.

Here, where once the Romans, looting and burning,
kindled profligate flames that left the whole   10
of Carthage nothing but a name alone,

love invades my thoughts, turning and returning,
to torture and set fire to the anxious soul,
and I in tears and ashes am undone.

Soneto XXXVII

Mi lengua va por do el dolor la guía;
ya yo con mi dolor sin guía camino;
entrambos hemos de ir con puro tino;
cada uno va a parar do no querría,

yo, porque voy sin otra compañía,   5
sino la que me hace el desatino;
ella, porque la lleve aquel que vino
a hacella decir más que querría.

Y es para mí la ley tan desigual,
que aunque inocencia siempre en mí conoce,   10
siempre yo pago el yerro ajeno y mío.

¿Qué culpa tengo yo del desvarío
de mi lengua, si estoy en tanto mal,
que el sufrimiento ya me desconoce?

Sonnet XXXVII

My tongue simply follows where pain leads,
while I with my pain am travelling in the dark;
both of us must find our way by guesswork,
both will arrive where we've no wish to be:

I, because there's none to guide my thought   5
but this foolishness that keeps me company,
she, because she's guided on her way
by one who made her say more than she ought.

And the law requires that I should come off worst,
for though my innocence is plain to see,   10
I pay for another's error and my own.

Why am I blamed when by my tongue alone
the fault's committed, being as I am so cursed
that suffering itself is loath to know me?

Anonymous engraving of the Danube, the site of Garcilaso's exile.

Songs

There are five *canciones* or songs (the Spanish equivalent of the Italian "canzoni"). I have included the third and the fifth, both more thoroughly Italianate than the others.

Song III can be clearly dated to around 1532, the year of Garcilaso's imprisonment on the island in the Danube that he describes. It emphasizes the contrast between the beauty and tranquillity of the speaker's surroundings and his actual mood and situation. His special sadness may have various causes. Perhaps it is unhappiness in love, something for which he expects to die, "something that's like death only much more harsh" (line 37). This is the conventional reason, laid down by the poetic tradition Garcilaso is following. Or perhaps it is the punishment he is undergoing, his confinement on the island in the Danube. But he appears both resigned to this and defiant: he can suffer no serious harm from one who has power over his body but none over his soul. He also implies that he is one who can bear it and who condemns himself, though in what way he condemns himself and exactly what for is not made clear. An overall cause for pessimism may be the collapse of his ambition to obtain advancement in the service of the emperor.

Whatever the main cause of Garcilaso's melancholy, he refers to it here in typically vague and indirect fashion, leaving us perhaps with a sense of something bigger that is not fully articulated. It is true that the speaker in the poem says that, if he dies, he does not want his death to be attributed to all his troubles together ("juntos tantos males," line 24), implying that this is what people may well think. In this he seems to be announcing his adherence to the literary convention of the lover dying for love. We may perhaps take it as a gesture of devotion not just to love, but to the poetic ideal he will follow and the new Italian style.

The image of flowing water accompanies the poem, both as an aspect of pastoral tranquillity and for its association with drowning and death; perhaps also the search for perfection in art is involved (compare the nymphs in Sonnet XI).

Like the other songs (but not Song V, the ode), he ends with an address to the song itself. The effect of personifying the song in this way may seem a little strange, but it is a convention, with precedent in Petrarch and followed later by Góngora in his *Second Solitude*.

The rhyme scheme is complex: *abcabccdeedff*. I have tried to give an idea of it with sound links (occasionally rhyme, but often very tenuous) in appropriate positions.

Song V, which Garcilaso wrote on behalf of his friend, the Italian poet Mario Galeota, is different from the others. It is really an ode, and has always been given the Latin title *Ode ad florem Gnidi*. Apparently Violante, Mario Galeota's love, was known in Naples as "the lily of Knidos or Nidos." Nidos was a district of Naples; spelt *Gnido* or *Cnidos* it recalls the shrine of Venus at Knidos. The name *lira*, taken from Garcilaso's opening line, was given to the poem's form, which was adopted by other golden age poets, most famously Luis de León and San Juan de la Cruz.

The poem's tone is also different: it is less personal, obviously, since there is no pretence that the poet is speaking for himself about his own love. This has led some readers to find it relatively cold and unemotional, but there are compensations, for example in the poem's greater clarity and its slight suggestion of humor. By comparison with Song III it seems like a step toward the more precise imagery of the eclogues. The poem starts by explicitly stating Garcilaso's intention not to write about war, but demonstrates that love too can be a source of conflict, violence, and tragedy. Seriousness however is dissipated by the humor and the use of expressions like "la concha de Venus," "Venus's shell," which have sexual connotations.

In terms of ideas the poem could be read as arguing the claims of lyric over epic poetry, and pointing toward the antimilitaristic theme Garcilaso develops in the elegies.

He directly states his interest in beauty over political power and military conquest, though expressing it in terms of power and relating it to the myth of Orpheus, symbolizing the power of art.

Canción III

Con un manso ruido
de agua corriente y clara,
cerca el Danubio una isla, que pudiera
ser lugar escogido
para que descansara   5
quien como yo estó agora, no estuviera;
do siempre primavera
parece en la verdura
sembrada de las flores;
hacen los ruiseñores   10
renovar el placer o la tristura
con sus blandas querellas,
que nunca día ni noche cesan dellas.

Aquí estuve yo puesto,
o por mejor decillo,   15
preso y forzado y solo en tierra ajena;
bien pueden hacer esto
en quien puede sufrillo
y en quien él a sí mismo se condena.
Tengo solo una pena,   20
Si muero desterrado
y en tanta desventura,
que piensen por ventura
que juntos tantos males me han llevado;
y sé yo bien que muero   25
por sólo aquello que morir espero.

Song III

With the gentle lapping
of limpid running water
the Danube surrounds an isle which surely would
be a perfect location
for someone (who was not as   5
I am now) to rest and restore his mood;
where eternal Spring's imbued
with an opulence of green
and profusion of flowers,
and every joy or sorrow's   10
reawakened by the nightingale's refrain,
repeating its soft complaint
day and night without ceasing for a moment.

Here I was posted,
or to speak more directly,   15
was held, imprisoned, alone on alien soil,
something easily foisted
on one able to bear it,
and who is first to put himself on trial.
I have one regret only: 20
if I die here, an exile,
and under an evil star,
they may think my troubles are
all of them together the cause, whereas I'll
know, as I take my last breath,   25
I die just for that from which I expect death.

El cuerpo está en poder
y en manos de quien puede
hacer a su placer lo que quisiere;
mas no podrá hacer   30
que mal librado quede,
mientras de mí otra prenda no tuviere.
Cuando ya el mal viniere
y la postrera suerte,
aquí me ha de hallar,   35
en el mismo lugar;
que otra cosa más dura que la muerte
me halla y ha hallado;
y esto sabe muy bien quien lo ha probado.

    No es necesario agora   40
hablar más sin provecho,
que es mi necesidad muy apretada;
pues ha sido en un hora
todo aquello deshecho
en que toda mi vida fué gastada.   45
Y al fin de tal jornada
¿presumen espantarme?
Sepan que ya no puedo
morir sino sin miedo;
que aun nunca qué temer quiso dejarme   50
la desventura mía,
que el bien y el miedo me quitó en un día.

    Danubio, río divino,
que por fieras naciones
vas con tus claras ondas discurriendo,   55
pues no hay otro camino
por donde mis razones
vayan fuera de aquí, sino corriendo
por tus aguas y siendo

My body is at the mercy
and in the possession
of one who can do whatever moves his heart;
but he will not have a way   30
to bring about my ruin
whose power has no hold on my other part.
And if the worst comes to pass,
the final throw of the dice,
it will find me as I am,   35
still here, just the same,
for something that's like death only much more harsh
has put me under its spell;
he who has had the experience knows it well.

So now there's no further need   40
for unprofitable talk;
the situation's too desperate, too fraught
since a single hour undid
the long years of work
to gain what my whole life passed in pursuit   45
of. After such a fight
do they think to scare me?
Know that I'll only be
able to die fearlessly,
for misfortune has left me nothing to fear: 50
it took all fear away
when it stole my happiness on the same day.

Sacred river Danube,
you who go among savage
nations, the flow of your clear waters guiding,   55
since there is no other route
by which my thoughts and my words
can go from this place, except by riding
your stream, or immersed in it

en ellas anegadas;   60
si en tierra tan ajena
en la desierta arena
fueren de alguno acaso en fin halladas,
entiérrelas, siquiera,
porque su error se acabe en tu ribera.   65

    Aunque en el agua mueras,
canción, no has de quejarte;
que yo he mirado bien lo que te toca.
Menos vida tuvieras
si hubieras de igualarte   70
con otras que se me han muerto en la boca.
Quién tiene culpa desto,
allá lo entenderás de mí muy presto.

and lost and drowned,   60
if in a foreign land
on the deserted strand
by some stranger they should finally be found,
let them be buried at least
and on your banks may their foolish wandering cease.   65

And if, my song, you die,
on flood waters, you've no cause
for complaint, I've looked after your needs;
you would have less life if I
had used you like others   70
that died without passing my lips. For this
who is to blame
you will hear soon when we meet beyond the stream.

Canción V
Ode ad florem Gnidi

Si de mi baja lira
tanto pudiese el son, que un momento
aplacase la ira
del animoso viento,
y la furia del mar y el movimiento;   5

y en ásperas montañas
con el suave canto enterneciese
las fieras alimañas,
los árboles moviese,
y al son confusamente los trajese;   10

no pienses que cantado
sería de mí, hermosa flor de Nido,
el fiero Marte airado,
a muerte convertido,
de polvo y sangre y de sudor teñido;   15

ni aquellos capitanes
en las sublimes ruedas colocados,
por quien los alemanes
el fiero cuello atados,
y los franceses van domesticados.   20

Mas solamente aquella
fuerza de tu beldad sería cantada,
y alguna vez con ella
también sería notada
el aspereza de que estás armada;   25

Song V
Ode ad florem Gnidi

If the sound of my simple
lyre had such power that in one moment
it could calm the anger
of the violent wind and
the fury of the sea, the sea's turbulence,   5

and if in the wilderness
with sweet singing I could melt the savage hearts
of the fiercest animals,
and so move the trees that
they approach, stirred and bewildered by the sound,   10

do not suppose, beautiful
lily of Knidos, that I would sing of
the deeds of angry Mars,
dedicated to death,
his countenance stained with powder, blood and sweat,   15

nor of the captains would I
sing, who ride in state, seated in high chariots,
by whom the German princes,
their proud necks tied to the yoke,
and French ones too, are tamed and put on show.   20

No, for I would sing of
nothing but the power of your beauty,
though occasionally too
I might put on record
the cold-heartedness which is your dread weapon,   25

y cómo por ti sola,
y por tu gran valor y hermosura,
convertida en viola,
llora su desventura
el miserable amante en su figura.   30

    Hablo de aquel cativo,
de quien tener se debe más cuidado,
que está muriendo vivo,
al remo condenado,
en la concha de Venus amarrado.   35

    Por ti, como solía,
del áspero caballo no corrige
la furia y gallardía,
ni con freno le rige,
ni con vivas espuelas ya le aflige.   40

    Por ti, con diestra mano
no revuelve la espada presurosa,
y en el dudoso llano
huye la polvorosa
palestra como sierpe ponzoñosa.   45

    Por ti, su blanda musa,
en lugar de la cítara sonante,
tristes querellas usa,
que con llanto abundante
hacen bañar el rostro del amante.   50

    Por ti, el mayor amigo
le es importuno, grave y enojoso;
yo puedo ser testigo,
que ya del peligroso
naufragio fuí su puerto y su reposo.   55

and tell how only through you,
for the sake of your quality, your beauty,
the wretched lover is turned
into a pale violet
your namesake, and weeps for his ill fortune.   30

It is of that captive
I speak who deserves more consideration,
for his is a living death,
sentenced and chained to the oar,
a slave caught and bound to the shell of Venus;   35

because of you, no longer
does he correct the fierce rebellion
of the restless stallion
or control him with the rein
or harry him with sharply pricking spurs;   40

because of you, he does not
brandish with expert skill the hasty sword,
and on the training ground
he flees the dusty lists
as if anxious to avoid a poisonous snake;   45

because of you, his gentle
muse abandons her sonorous lyre
for melancholy complaints,
which cause the lover's face
to be inundated with copious tears;   50

because of you, he finds
his best friend importunate, a bore, a burden;
as I can testify, who
once was in time of peril
and shipwreck his refuge and safe haven,   55

Y agora en tal manera
vence el dolor a la razón perdida,
que ponzoñosa fiera
nunca fué aborrecida
tanto como yo dél, ni tan temida.   60

No fuiste tú engendrada
ni producida de la dura tierra;
no debe ser notada
que ingratamente yerra
quien todo el otro error de sí destierra.   65

Hágate temerosa
el caso de Anajerete, y cobarde,
que de ser desdeñosa
se arrepintió muy tarde;
y así, su alma con su mármol arde.   70

Estábase alegrando
del mal ajeno el pecho empedernido,
cuando abajo mirando,
el cuerpo muerto vido
del miserable amante, allí tendido.   75

Y al cuello el lazo atado,
con que desenlazó de la cadena
el corazón cuitado,
que con su breve pena
compró la eterna punición ajena.   80

Sintió allí convertirse
en piedad amorosa el aspereza.
¡Oh tarde arrepentirse!
¡Oh última terneza!
¿Cómo te sucedió mayor dureza?   85

and now to such degree
is his lost reason overcome by grief
that no poisonous beast
was ever so much hated
as I by him, nor ever so much shunned.   60

You were not engendered from,
nor fashioned out of the hard earth; it is not
right that one should be known for
the sin of ingratitude,
who has banished from herself all other faults.   65

It were better you should fear
Anaxarete's outcome and avoid it,
who of her disdainfulness
too late repented and whose
soul therefore is burning with her marble flesh.   70

Her flinty heart exulted,
taking its pleasure in another's pain,
till chancing to turn her eyes
downward she saw the corpse
of the wretched lover stretched upon the ground,   75

and tied about his neck
the noose, by means of which he had released
the pained heart from its chains
and with this brief suffering
purchased another's lasting punishment.   80

Right there she felt her harshness
converted into tender loving pity.
O repentance come too late!
O tenderness at the last!
What then of the greater hardness soon to come?   85

Los ojos se enclavaron
en el tendido cuerpo que allí vieron,
los huesos se tornaron
más duros y crecieron,
y en sí toda la carne convirtieron;					90

las entrañas heladas
tornaron poco a poco en piedra dura;
por las venas cuitadas
la sangre su figura
iba desconociendo y su natura;					95

hasta que, finalmente,
en duro mármol vuelta y trasformada,
hizo de sí la gente
no tan maravillada
cuanto de aquella ingratitud vengada.					100

No quieras tú, señora,
de Némesis airada las saetas
probar, por Dios, agora;
baste que tus perfetas
obras y hermosura a los poetas					105

den inmortal materia,
sin que también en verso lamentable
celebren la miseria
de algún caso notable
que por ti pase triste y miserable.					110

Her eyes became fixed
on the lifeless body that they saw; then
her bones still further hardened
and grew, until they engrossed
all the flesh, taking it into themselves,   90

her frozen organs little
by little converted into solid stone;
in the anguished veins the blood
was beginning to forget
its proper form and function, its true nature;   95

until at the end she was
nothing but hard marble, metamorphosed,
and to the people less
a wonder to behold
than welcome proof of ingratitude avenged.   100

Do not you then, my lady,
tempt the arrows of angry Nemesis!
Avoid them for God's sake,
and let it be enough that
your perfect deeds, your beauty, should supply   105

the poets with immortal
inspiration, without their being obliged
in sad verses to record
some horrible disaster
laid at your door, some wretched tragedy.   110

The text on the plaque reads:

AQUÍ ESTÁN SEPULTADOS LOS RESTOS DEL EXIMIO VATE TOLEDANO
GARCILASO DE LA VEGA.
EXHUMADOS, EN 1869, PARA SER CONDUCIDOS AL PANTEÓN NACIONAL,
EL AMOR DE LA IMPERIAL CIUDAD REPRESENTADA POR
SU AYUNTAMIENTO, LOS RESTITUYÓ Á ESTE SARCÓFAGO FAMILIAR
EL DIA 17 DE AGOSTO DE 1900.
D. E. P.

The tomb of Garcilaso and his father at St. Peter the Martyr in Toledo, Spain.

Elegies and Epistle to Boscán

The two elegies, in *tercetos*, were written some time in 1535, after the Tunis campaign (see Sonnet XXXIII). The Epistle to Boscán is a little earlier, written most likely in the summer of 1534, when Garcilaso was returning to Naples after a mission to the court in Spain—probably to report the capture of Tunis by Barbarossa. All three poems are formally freer than Garcilaso's best-known work and in some sense more personal: they offer interesting insights into his situation and state of mind.

Elegy I commemorates Don Bernaldino, the duke of Alba's younger brother, who died of an illness at Trapani in Sicily. It can be a little confusing because it addresses different people at different times. I have supplied some breaks in the layout that are not present in the original, mainly to help identify the changes in the person addressed. Briefly, the opening addresses don Fernando, the present duke of Alba; lines 76–96 are a meditation on war; line 101 (English 102) shows that the poet has switched to addressing don Bernaldino, the dead brother; lines 130–80 speak of the mother and sisters, and then the river Tormes (personified) and nymphs and satyrs of the region, eventually urging the latter to stop mourning and try to console the family; line 181 returns to don Fernando, giving him reasons why he too should stop grieving. The end, from line 289, addresses don Bernaldino in heaven, promising that he will not be forgotten on earth (if heaven is kind enough to preserve the poet's work).

It may also be worth noting that the duke was a young man,

a little younger than Garcilaso, whose older friend Boscán had been his *ayo*, or "tutor," for manners and worldly accomplishments. It is written in terza rima, known in Spanish as *tercetos encadenados*, or "linked tercets." In my translation I have only sporadically attempted to reflect the rhyming, which in the Spanish gives to the form a certain tightness and unity that may seem lacking in the subject matter.

Elegy II, which is more of an epistle than an elegy and describes the poet's feelings about various aspects of his situation, refers explicitly to the period just after the North African campaign when the emperor's army was resting in Sicily before the return to Naples. It is also in written in tercets, and I have made a more sustained effort to follow the rhyme scheme in my translation.

The Epistle to Boscán follows the epistles of Horace and is the first poem in Spanish written in *endecasílabos sueltos*, or "blank verse" (though this equates it with the Latin hexameter rather than Elizabethan blank verse).

Elegía I

Al duque d'Alba en la muerte de don Bernaldino de Toledo

Aunque este grave caso haya tocado
con tanto sentimiento el alma mía,
que de consuelo estoy necesitado,
con que de su dolor mi fantasía
se descargase un poco, y se acabase   5
de mi continuo llanto la porfía,
    quise, pero, probar si me bastase
el ingenio a escribirte algún consuelo,
estando cual estoy, que aprovechase
    para que tu reciente desconsuelo   10
la furia mitigase, si las musas
pueden un corazón alzar del suelo
    y poner fin a las querellas que usas,
con que de Pindo ya las moradoras
se muestran lastimadas y confusas;   15
    que, según he sabido, ni a las horas
que el sol se muestra ni en el mar se esconde,
de tu lloroso estado no mejoras;
    antes en él permaneciendo, donde
quiera que estás tus ojos siempre bañas,   20
y el llanto a tu dolor así responde,
    que temo ver deshechas tus entrañas
en lágrimas, como al lluvioso viento
se derrite la nieve en las montañas.
    Si acaso el trabajado pensamiento   25
en el común reposo se adormece,
por tornar al dolor con nuevo aliento,
    en aquel breve sueño te aparece
la imagen amarilla del hermano,

Elegy I
To the duke of Alba on the death of don Bernaldino de Toledo

Although this dread event has touched my soul
with so deep a sadness that I feel
I myself have need of being consoled,
    in order to relieve my mind a little
of its burden and to stem the constant   5
flowing of my tears, I wanted still
    to write to you and try if I had the wit
to find for you some words of consolation,
something to help, despite my present state,
    calm the fury of your late affliction,   10
and see if the muses might be able
to raise a heart that's fallen to the ground
    and to those lamentations put a stop
which to the dwellers on Mount Pindos now
have become so painful, so disconcerting;   15
    for from what I've heard, neither when the sun
rises nor when it hides itself in the sea
do you manage to throw off your weeping fit
    but rather persist in it no matter where
you are, with eyes forever wet, with tears   20
responding so readily to grief I fear
    to see you internally dissolve in floods,
as when in Spring the mountain snows are melted
by the onset of the rainy warm west wind.
    Maybe it happens that the troubled mind   25
falls into a customary sleep before
returning with new energy to grieving
    and during that brief slumber the sallow
image of your brother appears to you,

que de la dulce vida desfallece;   30
    y tú, tendiendo la piadosa mano,
probando a levantar el cuerpo amado,
levantas solamente el aire vano;
    y del dolor el sueño desterrado
con ansia vas buscando, el que partido   35
era ya con el sueño y alongado.
    Así desfalleciendo en tu sentido,
como fuera de ti, por la ribera
de Trápana con llanto y con gemido
    el caro hermano buscas, que sola era   40
la mitad de tu alma, el cual muriendo,
no quedará ya tu alma entera.
    Y no de otra manera repitiendo
vas el amado nombre, en desusada
figura a todas partes revolviendo,   45
    que cerca del Erídano aquejada,
lloró y llamó Lampecia el nombre en vano,
con la fraterna muerte lastimada:
    "Ondas, tornadme ya mi dulce hermano
Faetón; si no, aquí veréis mi muerte,   50
regando con mis ojos este llano."
    ¡Oh cuántas veces, con el dolor fuerte
avivadas las fuerzas, renovaba
las quejas de su cruda y dura suerte!
    ¡Y cuántas otras, cuando se acababa   55
aquel furor, en la ribera umbrosa,
muerta, cansada, el cuerpo reclinaba!

    Bien te confieso que si alguna cosa
entre la humana puede y mortal gente
entristecer un alma generosa,   60
    con gran razón podrá ser la presente,
pues te ha privado de un tan dulce amigo,
no solamente hermano, un acidente;

as he fades and leaves the sweets of life behind,   30
    while you stretch forth your pitying hand and try
to raise the beloved body up again,
but what you raise is only empty air,
    and now with sleep quite banished by the pain
you desperately go searching for the one   35
who vanished with the dream and went away.
    Thus with your senses fainting and as if
beside yourself, you roam Trapani's shore,
weeping and groaning in your despair,
    and seek the dear lost brother who was half   40
of your own soul, which now that he is gone
will always lack the part that makes it whole;
    and thus you wander repeating the loved name,
turning in all directions, with the mad look,
of one who has quite lost his mind, like sad   45
    Lampetia when, weeping, she walked beside
the river Eridanus, calling in vain
the brother's name whose death so injured her:
    "Waves, give back to me my dear dead brother,
Phaethon; or be witnesses to my death,   50
as with my tears I water all this plain!"
    O, how many times spurred on by that sharp pain
she found new strength to shout out loud again
her complaints against the cruelty of harsh fate;
    and how many more, the storm having abated,   55
she lay her down on the shady river bank,
her poor body broken and exhausted!

    Confess to you I must that if there is
one thing that for us simple human mortals
can crush a generous heart and, with reason,   60
    teach despair, it is this that you have suffered,
because an accident has taken from you
not just a brother but also a dear friend,

el cual, no sólo siempre fue testigo
de tus consejos y íntimos secretos,   65
mas de cuanto lo fuiste tú contigo.
    En él se reclinaban tus discretos
y honestos pareceres, y hacían
conformes al asiento sus efetos.
    En él ya se mostraban y leían   70
tus gracias y virtudes una a una,
y con hermosa luz resplandecían,
    como en luciente de cristal coluna,
que no encubre de cuanto se avecina
a su viva pureza cosa alguna.   75

    ¡Oh, miserables hados! ¡Oh, mesquina
suerte la del estado humano, y dura,
do por tantos trabajos se camina!
    Y agora muy mayor la desventura
de aquesta nuestra edad, cuyo progreso   80
muda de un mal en otro su figura.
    ¿A quién ya de nosotros el eceso
de guerras, de peligros y destierro
no toca, y no ha cansado el gran proceso?
    ¿Quién no vió desparcir su sangre al hierro   85
del enemigo? ¿Quién no vió su vida
perder mil veces y escapar por yerro?
    ¿De cuántos queda y quedará perdida
la casa y la mujer y la memoria,
y de otros la hacienda despendida?   90
    ¿Qué se saca de aquesto? ¿Alguna gloria?
¿Algunos premios o agradecimientos?
Sabrálo quien leyere nuestra historia.
    Veráse allí que como polvo al viento,
así se deshará nuestra fatiga   95
ante quien se endereza nuestro intento.
    No contenta con esto la enemiga

who was privy not only to your counsels
and most intimate secrets but as well 65
to every thought that occupied your mind;
  in him were planted your wisest and most sincere
opinions, where they bore such fruit as
in that environment one might expect;
  in him could be seen and read your graces 70
and virtues, every one, and they shone out
with glorious light, like some radiant crystal
  column, of such a brilliance and purity
that it cannot be obscured or hidden
by anything in its vicinity. 75

  O wretched fate, unfortunate condition
that men are born to, and so laborious,
forcing them to travel such a weary road
  and now by how much greater the misfortune
of this our present age, which goes forward 80
changing its nature from one ill to another!
  Which of us now's not hurt by the excess
of wars, of danger and of banishment?
Who is not weary of the endless process?
  Who has not seen his blood spill on the blade 85
of his enemy? Who has not thought to die
a thousand times, and escaped by accident?
  How many have lost, will lose, their wife, their house
and their good name and how many others
will see their fortune plundered or dispersed? 90
  And for all this, what do we get? A little
glory? A prize, a word of gratitude?
He who reads our history will know the answer:
  there he will see how, like dust in the wind,
our hardships just dissolve and blow away 95
before Him toward whom all our efforts tend.
  And not content with this the enemy

del humano linaje, que invidiosa
coge sin tiempo el grano de la espiga,
   nos ha querido ser tan rigurosa, 100
que ni a tu juventud, don Bernaldino,
ni ha sido a nuestra pérdida piadosa.
   ¿Quién pudiera de tal ser adivino?
¿A quién no le engañara la esperanza,
viéndote caminar por tal camino? 105
   ¿Quién no se prometiera en abastanza
seguridad entera de tus años,
sin temer de natura tal mudanza?
   Nunca los tuyos, mas los propios daños,
dolernos deben; que la muerte amarga 110
nos muestra claros ya mil desengaños:
   hanos mostrado ya que en vida larga
apenas de tormentos y de enojos
llevar podemos la pesada carga;
   hanos mostrado en ti que claros ojos 115
y juventud y gracia y hermosura,
son también, cuando quiere, sus despojos.
   Mas no puede hacer que tu figura,
después de ser de vida ya privada,
no muestre el artificio de natura. 120
   Bien es verdad que no está acompañada
de la color de rosa que solía
con la blanca azucena ser mesclada;
   porque el calor templado que encendía
la blanca nieve de tu rostro puro, 125
robado ya la muerte te lo había.
   En todo lo demás, como en seguro
y reposado sueño descansabas,
indicio dando del vivir futuro.

   Mas ¿qué hará la madre que tú amabas, 130
de quien perdidamente eras amado,

of the human race, who in her envy
plucks the grain from the ear before it's ripe,
  has chosen to treat us so severely   100
that she has shown no mercy to your youth,
don Bernaldino, and for our loss no pity.
  Who could ever have prophesied this result?
Who not have been instead deceived by hope,
seeing your forward march along the route?   105
  or not have seen for you the ample promise
of a plenitude of fruitful years, rather
than fearing this reversal of nature's course?
  Not your misfortune but our own is what
we should lament, for already bitter death   110
is showing us a thousand disappointments;
  she has shown to us that we are scarcely able
to bear for the duration of a long life
our heavy load of torments and vexations;
  she has shown to us in you how she can make   115
bright eyes and youth, outstanding grace and beauty,
her prey whenever she should have a mind to.
  One thing, however, is beyond her power:
she cannot decree your form, even when life's
withdrawn, should not reveal the master hand   120
  of nature; true, it's not now accompanied
by the fresh pink that used to color it
mixed with the lily pallor of your skin,
  because the temperate heat that from within
lit the white snow of your unblemished cheek   125
death itself has already stolen from you;
  in all but this, as if in a secure
refreshing sleep you rested, giving proof
of the calm felicity of future life.

  But what will she do, the mother whom you loved,   130
by whom you were so desperately loved,

a quien la vida con la tuya dabas?
　　Aquí se me figura que ha llegado
de su lamento el son, que con su fuerza
rompe el aire vecino y apartado;　　　　　　135
　　tras el cual a venir también se esfuerza
el de las cuatro hermanas, que teniendo
va con el de la madre a viva fuerza.
　　A todas las contemplo desparciendo
de su cabello luengo el fino oro,　　　　　　140
al cual ultraje y daño están haciendo.
　　El viejo Tormes con el blanco coro
de sus hermosas ninfas seca el río,
y humedece la tierra con su lloro.
　　No recostado en urna al dulce frío　　　　145
de su caverna umbrosa, mas tendido
por el arena en el ardiente estío,
　　con ronco son de llanto y de gemido,
los cabellos y barbas mal paradas
se despedaza, y el sutil vestido.　　　　　　150
　　En torno dél sus ninfas, desmayadas,
llorando en tierra están sin ornamento,
con las cabezas de oro despeinadas.
　　Cese ya del dolor el sentimiento,
hermosas moradoras del undoso　　　　　　155
Tormes; tened más provechoso intento;
　　consolad a la madre, que el piadoso
dolor la tiene puesta en tal estado,
que es menester socorro presuroso.
　　Presto será que el cuerpo, sepultado　　160
en un perpetuo mármol, de las ondas
podrá de vuestro Tormes ser bañado.
　　Y tú, hermoso coro, allá en las hondas
aguas metido, podrá ser que al llanto
de mi dolor te muevas y respondas.　　　　165
　　Vos, altos promontorios, entre tanto

to whom it was your life that gave her hers?
Here where I am it seems to reach my ears,
the sound of her lamenting, so loud and strong
it rends the air close by and miles around;   135
    and behind it, also struggling to be heard,
comes that of the four sisters, in desperate
competition with the mother's keening.
    I see them all, as they in desolation
rend their fine gold hair, scattering the long   140
tresses, dishevelled and abused by grief.
    Old man Tormes, who with his pallid choir
of lovely nymphs has cried the river dry
and with this weeping flooded all the earth,
    no longer in the sweet cool of a shady   145
cavern leans on an urn, but lies prostrate
on burning sands in torrid summer heat;
    hoarse laments and groans are what he utters
and tears his unkempt hair and flimsy beard
and rips to shreds his insubstantial clothes;   150
    his fainting nymphs surround him, lost in grief,
trailing abandoned on the ground and shorn
of all adornment, golden hair uncombed.
    Enough, let these displays of sorrow cease,
fair inhabitants of rippling Tormes!   155
Take up some more productive course of action:
    try to console the mother, these mother's tears
have left her in so pitiful a state
she has right now most urgent need of help.
    It will not now be long before the body   160
rests beneath a tomb of lasting marble
and can be bathed by waters of your Tormes;
    and you, bright chorus, lying there submerged
in the deep waters, by my cry of pain
you will perhaps be moved and give some answer.   165
    Meanwhile, you high Trinacrian mountains,

con toda la Trinacria entristecida
buscad alivio en desconsuelo tanto.
Sátiros, faunos, ninfas, cuya vida
sin enojos se pasa, moradores   170
de la parte repuesta y escondida,
con luenga experiencia sabidores,
buscad para consuelo de Fernando
hierbas de propriedad oculta y flores;
así en el escondido bosque, cuando   175
ardiendo en vivo y agradable fuego
las fugitivas ninfas vais buscando,
ellas se inclinen al piadoso ruego,
y en recíproco lazo estén ligadas,
sin esquivar el amoroso juego.   180

Tú, gran Fernando, que entre tus pasadas
y tus presentes obras resplandeces,
y a mayor fama están por ti obligadas,
contempla dónde estás; que si falleces
al nombre que has ganado entre la gente,   185
de tu virtud en algo te enflaqueces.
Porque al fuerte varón no se consiente
no resistir los casos de fortuna
con firme rostro y corazón valiente.
Y no tan solamente esta importuna,   190
con proceso cruel y riguroso,
con revolver de sol, de cielo y luna,
mover no debe un pecho generoso,
ni entristecello con funesto vuelo,
turbando con molestia su reposo;   195
mas si toda la máquina del cielo
con espantable son y con ruído,
hecha pedazos, se viniere al suelo,
debe ser aterrado y oprimido
del grave peso y de la gran ruína,   200

together with all the saddened land, seek out
ways to relieve our overwhelming loss.
    You satyrs, fauns, and nymphs who pass your days
so happily free from care, inhabitants   170
of the most remote and secret, hidden regions,
    with the wisdom of your long experience
seek out to relieve Ferdinand's condition
herbs with hidden properties and flowers:
    thus, satyrs, in the heart of the forest when,   175
burning with quick and pleasurable fire,
you wander in pursuit of elusive nymphs,
    may they to your piteous pleas consent
and bind themselves to you reciprocally,
not hold themselves aloof from amorous play.   180

    And you, great Ferdinand whose light shines forth
amid the throng of your past and present deeds,
to which more fame is due because they're yours,
    consider your position, for if you betray
the reputation you have gained among   185
the people, you somewhat compromise your virtue,
    because to the strong man it is not permitted
that he should fail to meet adversity
with resolute countenance and valiant heart;
    and not only should it be impossible   190
for teasing Fortune with her pitiless ways,
her ever-turning sun and stars and moon,
    to undermine a generous heart's resolve
or darken it with the shadow of Death's wings,
with calamities unsettling its repose,   195
    but even if the whole machine of heaven
with the resounding din of its collapse
comes crashing down to shatter on the ground,
    better for him to be struck down and crushed
beneath the fearsome weight of the vast ruin,   200

primero que espantado y comovido.
Por estas asperezas se camina
de la inmortalidad al alto asiento,
do nunca arriba quien de aquí declina.

En fin, Señor, tornando al movimiento 205
de la humana natura, bien permito
a nuestra flaca parte un sentimiento;
mas el eceso en esto vedo y quito,
si alguna cosa puedo, que parece
que quiere proceder en infinito. 210
A lo menos el tiempo que, descrece
y muda de las cosas el estado,
debe bastar, si la razón fallece.
No fué el troyano príncipe llorado
siempre del viejo padre dolorido, 215
ni siempre de la madre lamentado;
antes, después del cuerpo redemido
con lágrimas humildes y con oro,
que fué del fiero Aquiles concedido,
y reprimido el lamentable coro 220
del frigio llanto, dieron fin al vano
y sin provecho sentimiento y lloro.
El tierno pecho, en esta parte humano,
de Venus, ¿qué sintió, su Adonis viendo
de su sangre regar el verde llano? 225
Mas des que vido bien que corrompiendo
con lágrimas sus ojos no hacía
sino en su llanto estarse deshaciendo,
y que tornar llorando no podía
su caro y dulce amigo de la escura 230
y tenebrosa noche al claro día,
los ojos enjugó, y la frente pura
mostró con algo más contentamiento,
dejando con el muerto la tristura;

than show any sign of terror and distress.
  Such is the hard road that must be travelled
to reach the high throne of immortality,
where one who strays from the way will not arrive.

  Finally, sir, returning to the motions   205
of human nature, I willingly allow
to our weaker part some sentiment, but still
    excess of it I'll prohibit and forbid,
if I have any say, for in this case
the grieving might go on eternally.   210
    Time, at any rate, which diminishes
all things and to all things brings alteration,
should serve the purpose, even if reason fails:
    the Trojan prince was not forever mourned
by his aged grief-stricken father, nor   215
was he lamented forever by his mother;
    rather, when the body had been ransomed,
which they had begged with humble tears and gold
till by fierce Achilles it was rendered up,
    the keening Trojan chorus repressed their tears,   220
bringing the vain and profitless expression
of sentiment and grief to a timely end.
    The tender heart of Venus, thus far human,
what did it feel when she saw Adonis
watering the green plain with his precious blood?   225
    Yet when she understood how ruining
her eyes with tears would do no more than spoil
her famous beauty and no way avail
    to bring her dear friend back, her sweet companion,
since no amount of crying could rescue him   230
from gloomy night and restore him to bright day,
    she wiped her eyes and smoothed her wondrous brow,
and putting on the appearance of composure,
left her grief behind with the dead boy.

y luego con gracioso movimiento   235
se fue su paso por el verde suelo,
con su guirnalda usada y su ornamento.
    Desordenaba con lacivo vuelo
el viento su cabello, y con su vista
alegraba la tierra, el mar y el cielo.   240
    Con discurso y razón que es tan prevista,
con fortaleza y ser que en ti contemplo,
a la flaca tristeza se resista.
    Tu ardiente gana de subir al templo
donde la muerte pierde su derecho,   245
te baste, sin mostrarte yo otro ejemplo.
    Allí verás cuán poco mal ha hecho
la muerte en la memoria y clara fama
de los famosos hombres que ha deshecho.
    Vuelve los ojos donde al fin te llama   250
la suprema esperanza, do perfeta
sube y purgada el alma en pura llama.
    ¿Piensas que es otro el fuego que en Oeta
de Alcides consumió la mortal parte
cuando voló el espiritu al alta meta?   255
    Desta manera aquel por quien reparte
tu corazón suspiros mil al día,
y resuena tu llanto en cada parte,
    subió por la dificil y alta vía,
de la carne mortal purgado y puro,   260
en la dulce región del alegría;
    do con discurso libre ya y seguro
mira la vanidad de los mortales,
ciegos, errados en el aire escuro;
    y viendo y contemplando nuestros males,   265
alégrase de haber alzado el vuelo
a gozar de las horas inmortales.
    Pisa el inmenso y cristalino cielo

And away with that gliding step of hers she sailed,   235
over the green, dressed and adorned as ever
with her customary garland and finery;
    the wind played wantonly with her wafted hair
and all creation, earth and sea and sky
was filled with gladness at the joyous vision.   240
    By rational thought and by farsighted reason,
by the fortitude and worth I know you have,
let debilitating grief be overcome.
    It is enough you have the burning wish
to mount to the temple where death will lose its rights;   245
you don't need other arguments from me.
    There you will see how little the effect
of death on the memory and the undimmed name
of all the famous men it has undone.
    Turn your eyes to that quarter where the supreme   250
hope beckons, where the soul is seen ascending
purged and perfected in the cleansing flame.
    Do you imagine it was any different,
that fire on Oeta which consumed the mortal
part of Hercules, when his spirit flew   255
    towards the high goal? That is how he for whom
your heart gives out a thousand sighs a day
and everywhere your weeping's to be heard
    has travelled by the difficult high path,
purified and purged of mortal flesh,   260
and entered the sweet region of delight,
    where now with independent and sure judgement
he sees the vanity of us mortal men,
as we wander, blind, in darkness, here below,
    and contemplating the evil that we do   265
and suffer, rejoices to have taken wing
and be able now to enjoy immortal life.
    The vast and crystalline sky is his domain,

teniendo puestos de una y otra mano
el claro padre y el sublime abuelo.   270
    El uno ve de su proceso humano
sus virtudes estar allí presentes,
que el áspero camino hacen llano;
    el otro, que acá hizo entre las gentes
en la vida mortal menor tardanza,   275
sus llagas muestra allá resplandecientes.
    (Dellas aqueste premio allá se alcanza;
porque del enemigo no conviene
procurar en el cielo otra venganza.)
    Mira la tierra, el mar que la contiene,   280
todo lo cual por un pequeño punto
a respeto del cielo juzga y tiene.
    Puesta la vista en aquel gran trasunto
y espejo, do se muestra lo pasado
con lo futuro y lo presente junto,   285
    el tiempo que a tu vida limitado
de allá arriba te está, Fernando, mira,
y allí ve tu lugar ya deputado.

    ¡Oh bienaventurado! que sin ira,
sin odio, en paz estás, sin amor ciego,   290
con quien acá se muere y se sospira;
    y en eterna holganza y en sosiego
vives, y vivirás cuanto encendiere
las almas del divino amor el fuego!
    Si el cielo piadoso y largo diere   295
luenga vida a la voz deste mi llanto,
lo cual tú sabes que pretende y quiere,
    yo te prometo, amigo, que entre tanto
que el sol al mundo alumbre, y que la escura
noche cubra la tierra con su manto,   300
    y en tanto que los peces la hondura

with his famous father seated on one hand
and on the other the marvellous grandfather: 270
    one surveys the march of his descendants
and sees the presence of his own virtues
making the rough road smooth; meanwhile the other,
    who made a shorter sojourn here on earth
and had less time among us mortal men,   275
displays his glorious wounds for admiration.
    (This is the prize he has been granted there,
because no other form of satisfaction
should you seek from your enemy in heaven.)
    He sees the earth and the sea containing it,   280
all which compared with heaven he adjudges
to be no more than a far-off tiny dot;
    fixing his gaze on that great book of records,
that mirror where the past is shown combined
with the future and the present all in one,   285
    he sees, great Ferdinand, the time allotted
to your life by heaven's ordinance, and sees
the place there that has been prepared for you.

    O happy you, free now from hate and anger,
who are at peace, and free from blind love also,   290
which we below ceaselessly die and sigh for,
    for there you live in perfect bliss, complete
repose, and will forever, while the fire
of divine love goes on inflaming souls!
    And if merciful, openhanded heaven gives   295
long life to this expression of my grief,
which as you know is what I hope and aim for,
    I promise you, my friend, for as long as
the sun continues to light the world and the dark
of night to draw across the earth its mantle,   300
    and while the fishes go on inhabiting

húmida habitarán del mar profundo,
y las fieras del monte la espesura,
    se cantará de ti por todo el mundo;
que en cuanto se discurre, nunca visto   305
de tus años jamás otro segundo
    será desde el Antártico a Calisto.

the deep sea's profound and watery depths,
and wild beasts roam the thickets on the mountain,
   you will be sung of everywhere in the world,
for say what they may, there never will be found   305
another of your years who is your equal,
from the Antarctic to the great Northern bear.

Elegía II
A Boscán

    Aquí, Boscán, donde del buen troyano
Anquises con eterno nombre y vida
conserva la ceniza el Mantuano,
    debajo de la seña esclarecida
de César Africano nos hallamos,   5
la vencedora gente recogida;
    diversos en estudio; que unos vamos
muriendo por coger de la fatiga
el fruto que con el sudor sembramos;
    otros, que hacen la virtud amiga   10
y premio de sus obras, y así quieren
que la gente lo piense y que lo diga,
    destotros en lo público difieren,
y en lo secreto sabe Dios en cuánto
se contradicen en lo que profieren.   15
    Yo voy por medio, porque nunca tanto
quise obligarme a procurar hacienda;
que un poco más que aquéllos me levanto.
    Ni voy tampoco por la estrecha senda
de los que cierto sé que a la otra vía   20
vuelven de noche, al caminar, la rienda.
    Mas, ¿dónde me llevó la pluma mía,
que a sátira me voy mi paso a paso,
y aquesta que os escribo es elegía?
    Yo enderezo, señor, en fin, mi paso   25
por donde vos sabéis, que su proceso
siempre ha llevado y lleva Garcilaso;
    y así, en mitad de aqueste monte espeso
de las diversidades me sostengo,

Elegy II
To Boscán

Here, Boscán, where the great Mantuan locates
the ashes of old Anchises, the illustrious
Trojan, whose name and fame he celebrates,
    all of us are gathered under the glorious
banners of the present-day African   5
Caesar, we who returned victorious;
    but we differ in our aims, for some can
hardly wait to gather in the harvest,
to reap the crop that with our sweat was sown,
    while others, who say that virtue is their friend   10
and only recompense for all their efforts,
hoping people will believe it and commend
    them, publicly differ from the first lot,
although in private God knows to what extent
what they profess goes counter to their true thought.   15
    I take the middle way, for I've never meant
to push myself so much in pursuit of wealth:
I aim a little higher than all that.
    Nor do I wish to follow the narrow path
of those who I'm sure reverse their route at night,   20
turning their horses' heads from north to south.
    But the way my pen is taking me's not right,
for step-by-step I'm heading towards satire,
when it's meant to be an elegy I write.
    Finally, now, I shall redirect my steps, sir,   25
in a direction that, as you well know,
always has been, and still is, Garcilaso's;
    for in this dense forest variousness is how
I find a way to manage what life chooses

no sin dificultad, mas no por eso 30
   dejo las musas, antes torno y vengo
dellas al negociar, y variando,
con ellas dulcemente me entretengo.
   Así se van las horas engañando,
así del duro afán y grave pena 35
estamos algún hora descansando.
   De aquí iremos a ver de la Sirena
la patria, que bien muestra haber ya sido
de ocio y de amor antiguamente llena.
   Allí mi corazón tuvo su nido 40
un tiempo ya; mas no sé ¡triste! Agora
o si estará ocupado o desparcido.
   De aquesto un frío temor así a deshora
por mis huesos discurre en tal manera,
que no puedo vivir con él un hora. 45
   Si ¡triste! de mi bien estado hubiera
un breve tiempo ausente, yo no niego
que con mayor seguridad viviera.
   La breve ausencia hace el mismo juego
en la fragua de amor, que en fragua ardiente 50
el agua moderada hace al fuego;
   la cual verás que no tan solamente
no lo suele matar, mas lo refuerza
con ardor más intenso y eminente;
   porque un contrario con la poca fuerza 55
de su contrario, por vencer la lucha,
su brazo aviva y su valor esfuerza;
   pero si el agua en abundancia mucha
sobre el fuego se esparce y se derrama,
el humo sube al cielo, el son se escucha, 60
   y el claro resplandor de viva llama,
en polvo y en ceniza convertido,
apenas queda dél sino la fama.
   Así el ausencia larga, que ha esparcido

for me; not easy, it's true, but even so   30
   I have no thought of giving up the Muses:
I turn from them to business, but gratefully
return to their company, which amuses
   me. Thus the hours keep passing, deceptively;
thus from hard work and serious concerns   35
we find some chance to escape and take it easy.
   When we move from here, our company returns
to the land of the Siren, which from of old
has been a place of love and sweet diversions.
   There my heart was previously consoled   40
by having a nest, but sadly now who knows
if I'll not find it taken or despoiled.
   From this idea, unbidden, a cold fear grows
and spreads throughout my bones in such a style
it allows me not one moment of repose.   45
   Had I been absent only for a short spell
there would be, I'm sure, less cause for my unease
and I would have more confidence as well:
   a short absence will in love's furnace cause
the same effect as in the blacksmith's forge   50
a little water has on the fire, which roars
   louder, instead of dying, with the urge
to renew itself, the water only serving
as stimulus to intensify its rage,
   like an adversary who, observing   55
the other's weakness, sees himself soon victor,
and summons all his strength for the final fling.
   But when a greater quantity of water
is spread or cast upon the blazing coals,
the smoke and din born of this encounter   60
   rise to heaven, the fiery splendor pales
and what was living flame is now only
dust and ashes, scarcely anything remains
   but its memory: just so does a lengthy

en abundancia su licor, que amata   65
el fuego que el amor tenía encendido,
    de tal suerte lo deja, que lo trata
la mano sin peligro en el momento
que en aparencia y son se desbarata.

    Yo sólo fuera voy de aqueste cuento;   70
porque el amor me aflige y me atormenta,
y en el ausencia crece el mal que siento;
    y pienso yo que la razón consienta
y permita la causa deste efeto,
que a mí solo entre todos se presenta;   75
    porque, como del cielo yo sujeto
estaba eternamente y deputado
al amoroso fuego en que me meto,
    así para poder ser amatado,
el ausencia sin término infinita   80
debe ser, y sin tiempo limitado;
    lo cual no habrá razón que lo permita;
porque, por más y más que ausencia dure,
con la vida se acaba, que es finita.
    Mas a mí ¿quién habrá que me asegure   85
que mi mala fortuna con mudanza
y olvido contra mí no se conjure?
    Este temor persigue la esperanza
y oprime y enflaquece el gran deseo
con que mis ojos van de su holganza.   90
    Con ellos solamente agora veo
este dolor que el corazón me parte,
y con él y comigo aquí peleo.
    ¡Oh crudo, oh riguroso, oh fiero Marte,
de túnica cubierto de diamante,   95
y endurecido siempre en toda parte!
    ¿Qué tiene que hacer el tierno amante
con tu dureza y áspero ejercicio
llevado siempre del furor delante?

absence pour water on love's flame to end it,   65
leaving the fire that burned before so brightly
   in such a state it's even safe to handle,
now that its former vigor and brilliance fail
and all the noise and signs of burning dwindle.
   I am the one exception to this rule,   70
for I still suffer love's fatigues and torments,
and absence only increases the pain I feel;
   and I believe that reason still assents,
and tolerates the cause of this effect,
which to me alone among men presents   75
   itself, because it seems I'm always subject—
committed by heaven before time began—
to love's fire, which willingly I enter:
   this is the burning fire that only can
be put out by an absence with no limit,   80
an absence infinite, without return,
   something reason anyway cannot permit,
for however long an absence may endure,
it still must end with life and life is finite.
   But how could anyone ever make me sure   85
that against happiness my wretched fortune
will not with change and neglectfulness conspire?
   Hope is banished by this apprehension,
repressed and weakened too the strong desire
that points my eyes the way to what delights them: 90
   all they discover now, no matter where
I turn them, is this pain that splits my heart;
with it and with myself I am at war.
   Oh cruel, fearsome and relentless Mars,
protected by your adamantine tunic,   95
always impervious in every part!
   What has the tender lover to do with
your callousness and savage occupation,
unceasingly spurred on by a mad fury?

Ejercitando, por mi mal, tu oficio,   100
soy reducido a términos que muerte
será mi postrimero beneficio.

Y ésta no permitió mi dura suerte
que me sobreviniese peleando,
de hierro traspasado agudo y fuerte,   105
por que me consumiese contemplando
mi amado y dulce fruto en mano ajena,
y el duro posesor de mí burlando.
Mas, ¿dónde me trasporta y enajena
de mi proprio sentido el triste miedo?   110
A parte de vergüenza y dolor llena,
donde si el mal yo viese, ya no puedo,
según con esperalle estoy perdido,
acrecentar en la miseria un dedo.
Así lo pienso agora, y si él venido   115
fuese en su misma forma y su figura,
tendría el presente por mejor partido,
y agradecería siempre a la ventura
mostrarme de mi mal sólo el retrato,
que pintan mi temor y mi tristura.   120
Yo sé qué cosa es esperar un rato
el bien del propio engaño, y solamente
tener con él inteligencia y trato.
Como acontece al mísero doliente,
que del un cabo el cierto amigo y sano   125
le muestra el grave mal de su acidente,
y le amonesta que del cuerpo humano
comience a levantar a mejor parte
el alma suelta con volar liviano;
mas la tierna mujer, de la otra parte,   130
no se puede entregar a desengaño,
y encúbrele del mal la mayor parte;
él, abrazado con su dulce engaño,
vuelve los ojos a la voz piadosa,

Summoned, alas, to practice your profession,   100
I am reduced to such a state that death will
seem to me a final benediction.

And here again I have to blame my ill
fortune, that did not let death come to me
in battle, on the foe's sharp iron bill,   105

preferring instead to make me live to see
my beloved prize clasped in another's arms,
and the cruel dispossessor mocking me.

But where am I taken by these sad alarms
divided from myself and all good sense?   110
To a place full of misery and shame,

where, should I meet the worst, there's yet no chance—
since by just thinking it I am undone—
it can add to my weight of misery one ounce.

I say this now, but if it should truly happen   115
in the very shape of my imagining,
I would think my present state the better bargain

and bless my luck if it should show me nothing
but this gloomy portrait of my ruin
painted by my fear and my despairing.   120

I know well what it is to put one's faith in
the happiness that comes from self-deception,
and to have no truck with any other version.

Thus it is with the sick man who has one
true and faithful friend, willing to show him   125
the mortal gravity of his condition,

and remind him of his duty to begin
to release the soul from its corporeal bond
and free it for the soaring flight to heaven;

the tender-hearted wife on the other hand   130
conceals from him the truth about his state,
having no heart to make him understand;

embracing eagerly the sweet deceit,
he turns his eyes toward the gentle voice,

y alégrase muriendo con su daño,   135
    así los quito yo de toda cosa,
y póngolos en solo el pensamiento
de la esperanza cierta o mentirosa.
    En este dulce error muero contento;
porque ver claro y conocer mi estado   140
no puede ya curar el mal que siento;
    y acabo como aquel que en un templado
baño metido, sin sentido muere,
las venas dulcemente desatado.

    Tú, que en la patria entre quien bien te quiere   145
la deleitosa playa estás mirando,
y oyendo el son del mar que en ella hiere,
    y sin impedimento contemplando
la misma a quien tú vas eterna fama,
en tus vivos escritos, procurando;   150
    alégrate, que más hermosa llama
que aquella que el troyano encendimiento
pudo causar, el corazón te inflama.
    No tienes que temer el movimiento
de la fortuna con soplar contrario,   155
que el puro resplandor serena el viento.
    Yo, como conducido mercenario,
voy do fortuna a mi pesar me envía,
si no a morir, que aquesto es voluntario.
    Sólo sostiene la esperanza mía   160
un tan débil engaño, que de nuevo
es menester hacello cada día;
    y si no lo fabrico y lo renuevo,
da consigo en el suelo mi esperanza;
tanto, que en vano a levantalla pruebo.   165
    Aqueste premio mi servir alcanza,
que en sola la miseria de mi vida
negó fortuna su común mudanza.

and meets death unaware, to his soul's hurt: 135
    so do I close my eyes, of my own choice,
to all but the thoughts of hope, and so do I
not care whether the hope be true or false;
    in this sweet error I am content to die,
because to recognize my true condition   140
can no longer remedy the pain that I
    experience; and I end just like the one
who in a warm bath opens up a vein,
and, feeling nothing, softly passes on.

    You, who stand gazing at that enchanting view   145
of the sea, and hear waves beating on the shore,
in your native land, among those who love you,
    unhindered in your contemplation of her
whose eternal fame you've set out to procure
in the brilliant writings that embody her,   150
    rejoice, for a flame that rises even higher
than that which led to the burning down of Troy
fills your heart with the beauty of its fire;
    no need for you to fear the inconstancy
of fortune, its sharp winds blowing counter,   155
for the purity of that shining calms the sea.
    I, a driven mercenary, am bound to
go where fortune sends me, against my will,
unless to death, which gladly I agree to.
    Only by a deceit so tenuous and frail   160
that it has to be renewed again each day
can I sustain the hope that keeps me whole;
    and if I don't renew it, I will pay
dearly, as my hopes come crashing to the ground,
for to raise them after that I'll find no way.   165
    My service gains me only this reward:
that fortune denies her wonted fickleness,
in guaranteeing my life is always hard.

¿Dónde podré huir que sacudida
un rato sea de mí la grave carga   170
que oprime mi cerviz enflaquecida?
    Mas ¡ay! Que la distancia no descarga
el triste corazón, y el mal, doquiera
que estoy, para alcanzarme el vuelo alarga.
    Si donde el sol ardiente reverbera   175
en la arenosa Libia, engendradora
de toda cosa ponzoñosa y fiera;
    o adonde es él vencido a cualquiera hora
de la rígida nieve y viento frío,
parte do no se vive ni se mora;   180
    si en ésta o en aquélla el desvarío
o la fortuna me llevase un día,
y allí gastase todo el tiempo mío;
    el celoso temor con mano fría
en medio del calor y ardiente arena   185
el triste corazón me apretaría;
    y en el rigor del hielo, en la serena
noche, soplando el viento agudo y puro,
que el veloce correr del agua enfrena,
    de aqueste vivo fuego en que me apuro   190
y consumirme poco a poco espero,
sé que aun allí no podré estar seguro;
    y así, diverso entre contrarios muero.

Where can I flee to, in what resting-place
for a while shake off the heavy yoke that bows   170
my weakened neck and find a breathing-space?
    Distance, alas, to the sad heart allows
no relief: this pain, wherever I may wander,
reaches out and catches me by the heels.
    Supposing that to Libya, progenitor   175
of fierce and venomous things of every kind,
where the blazing sun beats down on the desert or
    to some land where by the rigor of cold wind
and snow the sun is always overcome,
some place where nothing living can reside,   180
    suppose, one day, to one or the other clime,
I should be by madness or by fortune led,
there to use up all my allotted time,
    jealousy would still with a hand that's cold
even amid the burning desert sands   185
reach in and crush my tired heart in its hold;
    and in the severity of frozen lands
where night air freezes and wind is sharp enough
to hold swift-flowing water in icy bands,
    even there I know there's no escape   190
from this living fire by which I'm mortified,
this fire which little by little eats me up,
so divided between contraries I die.

Epístola a Boscán

Señor Boscán, quien tanto gusto tiene
de daros cuenta de los pensamientos
hasta en las cosas que no tienen nombre,
no le podrá con vos faltar materia,
ni será menester buscar estilo   5
presto, distinto, de ornamento puro,
tal cual a culta epístola conviene.
    Entre muy grandes bienes que consigo
el amistad perfeta nos concede,
es aqueste descuido suelto y puro   10
lejos de la curiosa pesadumbre;
y así, de aquesta libertad gozando,
digo que vine, cuanto a lo primero,
tan sano como aquel que en doce días
lo que sólo veréis ha caminado   15
cuando el fin de la carta os lo mostrare.
    Alargo y suelto a su placer la rienda,
mucho más que al caballo, al pensamiento,
y llévame a las veces por camino
tan dulce y agradable, que me hace   20
olvidar el trabajo del pasado.
Otras me lleva por tan duros pasos,
que con la fuerza del afán presente,
también de los pasados se me olvida.
A veces sigo un agradable medio   25
honesto y reposado en que el discurso
del gusto y del ingenio se ejercita.
    Iba pensando y discurriendo un día
a cuántos bienes alargó la mano

Epistle to Boscán

Señor Boscán, for one who takes such pleasure
in telling you whatever he is thinking,
including things that do not have a name,
there never can be any lack of subjects,
nor does he need to search for a lively,⁣ 5
lucid, chastely embellished style, such as
would befit a learned composition.
Not least among the benefits that perfect
friendship confers on us is this relaxed
and unpretentious carelessness, so far 10
removed from anything contrived or pompous;
so, taking advantage of this freedom,
I shall say, as to my subject, that I arrived
as fit as one can be who in twelve days
has travelled what distance you will discover, 15
but only when the letter's end informs you.
I give free rein not only to my horse,
but also, more importantly, to my thought,
which sometimes carries me along a road
so sweet and pleasant it leads me to forget 20
all the previous hardships of the journey;
at other times it gives me so rough a ride
that in my struggle with these present trials,
I also forget about what went before;
sometimes I take a pleasant middle way, 25
straightforward and serene, where one's thoughts run
on the pleasures of poetic style and wit.
One day as I went I was considering
what great benefits were made available

el que de la amistad mostró el camino;						30
y luego vos, de la amistad ejemplo,
os me ofrecéis en estos pensamientos.
Y con vos a lo menos me acontece
una gran cosa, al parecer estraña;
y porque la sepáis en pocos versos,						35
es que, considerando los provechos,
las honras y los gustos que me vienen
desta vuestra amistad, que en tanto tengo,
ninguna cosa en mayor precio estimo,
ni me hace gustar del dulce estado,						40
tanto como el amor de parte mía.
Este conmigo tiene tanta fuerza,
que sabiendo muy bien las otras partes
de la amistad, de la estrecheza nuestra,
con sólo aqueste el alma se enternece;						45
y sé que otra mente me aprovecha,
que el deleite, que suele ser pospuesto
a las útiles cosas y a las graves.
Llévame a escudriñar la causa desto
ver contino tan recio en mí el efeto,						50
y hallo que el provecho, el ornamento,
el gusto y el placer que se me sigue
del vínculo de amor que nuestro genio
enredó sobre nuestros corazones,
son cosas que de mí no salen fuera,						55
y en mí el provecho sólo se convierte.
Mas el amor, de donde por ventura
nacen todas las cosas, si hay alguna,
que a vuestra utilidad y gusto miren,
es razón grande que en mayor estima						60
tenido sea de mí, que todo el resto,
cuánto más generosa y alta parte
es el hacer el bien que el recebillo;
así que amando me deleito, y hallo

by the one who taught us friendship's proper path,   30
and just then you, as a living example,
came unannounced into these thoughts of mine;
for with you at least there's something special
that happens to me, seemingly quite strange,
and, to put it briefly in few verses,   35
it is this: if I consider the profit,
the honor and the pleasure I derive
from this friendship with you, which I so prize,
there is nothing I esteem more highly, or
that puts me in a greater state of rapture,   40
than the love that from myself I give to you.
So much power does this love have for me
that knowing full well the other aspects
of friendship and of our intimacy,
this alone is enough to move my soul,   45
and the delight that usually comes second
to things considered useful and more serious,
profits me I am sure quite differently.
I am impelled to seek the cause of this
because I see the effect in me so strong,   50
and I find the advantage, the distinction,
the pleasure and enjoyment that result
from the bond of love woven by our natures
to involve our hearts and bind them into one,
are things that go nowhere outside of me—   55
the profit from them is for me alone.
But this love, from which perhaps are born
all the things—assuming that there be some—
that tend toward your benefit and pleasure,
is something that with good reason I can hold   60
in greater esteem than all the rest, because
it is so much better and more generous
to do good to another than receive it;
thus, loving, I experience delight

que no es locura este deleite mío.   65
¡Oh cuán corrido estoy y arrepentido
de haberos alabado el tratamiento
del camino de Francia y las posadas!
Corrido de que ya por mentiroso
con razón me tendréis; arrepentido   70
de haber perdido tiempo en alabaros
cosa tan dina de vituperio;
donde no hallaréis sino mentiras,
vinos acedos, camareras feas,
varletes codiciosos, malas postas,   75
gran paga, poco argén, largo camino;
llegar al fin a Nápoles no habiendo
dejado allá enterrado algún tesoro,
salvo si no decís que es enterrado
lo que nunca se halla ni se tiene.   80
A mi señor Durall estrechamente
abrazad de mi parte, si pudierdes.
Doce del mes de Otubre, de la tierra
do nació el claro fuego del Petrarca,
y donde están del fuego las cenizas.   85

and this delight I hold to be no madness.   65
    Oh, how ashamed I am, how I regret
having praised to you the service one receives
on the roads of France and at the wayside inns!
Ashamed because you now, and with good reason,
will take me for a liar; regretful   70
that I wasted so much time in praising
that which is worthy rather of harsh censure,
for there you will find nothing else but lies,
vinegar for wine, ugly waitresses,
greedy servants, execrable stables,   75
high prices, little money, a long road;
at best, to come to Naples finally,
not having left there a buried treasure,
unless you want to call that buried which
one's never going to find or to enjoy!   80
Give to our friend Durall a close embrace
from me, that is, if you can find a way to.
Dated the twelfth day of October, from
the place where Petrarch's flame of love was lit,
and where the ashes of that fire are saved.   85

Anonymous engraving of Don Pedro de Toledo (sixteenth century?).

Eclogues

The three eclogues were written during the Naples period. I have kept them in the traditional order, though rather confusingly Eclogue II was written first. The word "eclogue" was used in the Renaissance to refer to a short poem imitated from Virgil with a pastoral or bucolic subject. Garcilaso's contain some passages that quite closely resemble passages in Virgil. All three eclogues list the characters at the beginning, but Eclogue II alone is presented through dialogue and shows other signs of dramatic structure. The others are introduced by a narrator.

Eclogue I is dedicated to don Pedro de Toledo, Viceroy of Naples and uncle of the Duke of Alba. It is actually the second of the eclogues, written later than Eclogue II. It has a complicated rhyme scheme, which I have not tried to follow, but I have kept to the pattern of long and short lines (in the original, hendecasyllables and heptasyllables).

After the dedication, the speaker sets the pastoral scene: the sun is rising on a typically idyllic setting, a tall tree, greenery, the sound of water. First Salicio sings of his pain at being abandoned for another by the woman he loves, then Nemoroso sings of his grief at the death of the woman he loves. A final stanza describes the sun setting, as shepherds and sheep wend their way home.

There is no attempt to give the shepherds distinct characters or realistic speech (this is no shepherds' play). But Garcilaso does link feelings and setting with some degree of realism. Salicio feels he does not deserve to be jilted when he has fresh milk in abundance and a large flock. His sheep may be bred from Virgil's or Sannazaro's but they are Spanish sheep: they undergo the *trashumación*, the summer and winter migration between Extremadura and the mountains of Cuenca. For both men the fact that in a happier past they enjoyed nature in the company of the woman they loved makes nature now a sad reminder of happiness departed.

In Eclogue II, which has a total of 1,885 lines, I have made extensive cuts, but I have tried to provide enough to allow comparison with the other eclogues. There are really two parts: a narrative, concerning Albanio's unhappy love, and a history of the house of Alba. I have abridged the narrative and excluded the entire second part. The whole eclogue is written in a variety of verse forms, including a long section with internal rhyme. It is also a mixture of genres, the history of the house of Alba being Garcilaso's nearest approach to epic.

There is no dedication in Eclogue II and no narrator. It begins directly with Albanio speaking of his unhappiness in love and continues with interventions by his friends, Salicio and later Nemoroso. The lack of a narrator presupposes some attempt at dramatization, but long unrealistic expositions are needed, with Albanio first speaking in soliloquy and then describing to Salicio how he fell in love with Camila, and the disastrous consequences of revealing his feelings to her. About halfway through there is a confrontation between Albanio and Camila, the woman he loves, where there is genuine dramatic dialogue, some of it comic, and in the later scene of Albanio's madness, observed by Salicio and Nemoroso, it is quite natural for him (as a madman) to be talking to himself, or to his reflection in the water.

Leaving aside the question of its dramatic form, the poem does show a definite interest in the psychology of love, taking it beyond mere poetic convention. Albanio's conventional role of scorned victim in relation to Camila changes to one of potential aggressor when he comes upon her sleeping. There is some evidence to suggest that he deserves his unhappy fate, since he has very little apprehension of Camila as an independent person, despite the adulation of her tomboyish personality and hunting skills in the first part of the poem.

Water, as so often in Garcilaso, plays an important part. The spring described by Albanio at the opening is associated with his adolescence and the birth of his love, and also with the disastrous moment when he makes it known and with the occasion when she returns and he catches her sleeping. Later she calls on the spring as witness of what he did and finally it becomes a mirror in which like Narcissus he views himself.

There have been suggestions that this eclogue might have been performed and we may wonder if Garcilaso might have moved further in the direction of drama, and perhaps comedy, had he lived longer. From the evidence of the other eclogues, however, he was moving in the opposite direction.

Eclogue III is Garcilaso's last poem, and it is thought that it still awaited a final revision at the time of his death. It is written in *octava real*, and I have attempted, where possible, to follow the rhyme scheme (*ababacc*).

For me, the introductory dedication breathes the spirit of someone confident of his position and his poetic skills, which have found an appreciative audience among friends who love and admire him. It also reveals indirectly some of his concerns, particularly the difficulty of reconciling the various demands on his time.

The grief that permeated the first eclogue is still present, but here subordinated to the serene beauty of the classical vision.

Egloga I
Al virrey de Napoles
Personas: Salicio, Nemoroso

El dulce lamentar de dos pastores,
Salicio juntamente y Nemoroso,
he de contar, sus quejas imitando;
cuyas ovejas al cantar sabroso
estaban muy atentas, los amores,   5
de pacer olvidadas, escuchando.
Tú, que ganaste obrando
un nombre en todo el mundo,
y un grado sin segundo,
agora estés atento, sólo y dado   10
al ínclito gobierno del Estado
albano; agora vuelto a la otra parte,
resplandeciente, armado,
representando en tierra el fiero Marte;

agora de cuidados enojosos   15
y de negocios libre, por ventura
andes a caza, el monte fatigando
en ardiente jinete, que apresura
el curso tras los ciervos temerosos,
que en vano su morir van dilatando;   20
espera, que en tornando
a ser restituído
al ocio ya perdido,
luego verás ejercitar mi pluma
por la infinita innumerable suma   25
de tus virtudes y famosas obras;
antes que me consuma,
faltando a ti, que a todo el mundo sobras.

Eclogue I

To the viceroy of Naples
Personae: Salicio, Nemoroso

Of two shepherds' melodious laments,
Salicio's and also Nemoroso's,
I shall sing, reproducing their complaints;
to that delicious song the curious sheep
listened, forgetful of the joys of feeding,   5
while they attended to the tale of love.
   You, who through your deeds have earned
   a worldwide reputation
   and title beyond compare,
whether at this moment given over   10
entirely to the government of your realm
of Alba, or whether engaged elsewhere
   resplendent in your armor,
taking the warlike role of Mars on earth,

or if, finding yourself free from tedious cares   15
and troublesome affairs of state, perhaps
you have gone hunting, wearing out the mountains
on a fiery thoroughbred, pressing hard
after the stag, which flees with the vain hope
of delaying its inevitable death,   20
   please wait, for when my absent
   leisure is restored to me
   and I have the time for it,
you will see how immediately my pen
takes up the task of listing the infinite   25
number of your virtues and your exploits,
   for fear I might die too soon,
and sell you short, who over the world excel.

En tanto que este tiempo que adivino
viene a sacarme de la deuda un día,   30
que se debe a tu fama y a tu gloria;
que es deuda general, no sólo mía,
mas de cualquier ingenio peregrino
que celebra lo dino de memoria;
el árbol de vitoria   35
que ciñe estrechamente
tu gloriosa frente
dé lugar a la hiedra que se planta
debajo de tu sombra, y se levanta
poco a poco, arrimada a tus loores;   40
y en cuanto esto se canta,
escucha tú el cantar de mis pastores.

Saliendo de las ondas encendido,
rayaba de los montes el altura
el sol, cuando Salicio, recostado   45
al pie de un alta haya, en la verdura,
por donde un agua clara con sonido
atravesaba el fresco y verde prado;
él, con canto acordado
al rumor que sonaba,   50
del agua que pasaba,
se quejaba tan dulce y blandamente
como si no estuviera de allí ausente
la que de su dolor culpa tenía;
y así, como presente,   55
razonando con ella, le decía.

Salicio
¡Oh más dura que mármol a mis quejas,
y al encendido fuego en que me quemo
más helada que nieve, Galatea!

And until that time, which as I foresee
will come one day to relieve me of the debt   30
that's owed to your great fame and to your glory
(the debt of all the world, not only mine
but that of every man of rare intellect,
who celebrates things worthy of recording),
    let the branch of victory   35
    that is so firmly bound
    about your glorious brow
make way for the ivy, which is growing
in your shadow and gradually ascending
little by little, leaning on your fame,   40
    and until that glory's sung,
listen to the singing of my shepherds.

The sun was just emerging from the waves,
already ablaze, flooding the mountain tops
with light, when Salicio, stretched out on the ground   45
at the foot of a tall beech in a green spot,
where a tinkling stream of crystal water
ran laughing through the grass of a green meadow,
    began to sing, in accord
    with the gentle sound   50
    of running water,
a plaintive song, so sweet, so soft and gentle
it seemed she was not absent from that place,
who was responsible for all his pain,
    and, just as if she stood there,   55
he laid his thoughts before her, sadly saying:

Salicio
O harder than marble to my complaints,
and to the raging fire with which I burn
colder than freezing snow, O Galatea!

Estoy muriendo, y aún la vida temo;   60
témola con razón, pues tú me dejas;
que no hay, sin ti, el vivir para qué sea.
Vergüenza he que me vea
ninguno en tal estado,
de ti desamparado,   65
y de mí mismo yo me corro agora.
¿De un alma te desdeñas ser señora,
donde siempre moraste, no pudiendo
della salir un hora?
Salid sin duelo, lágrimas, corriendo.   70

El sol tiende los rayos de su lumbre
por montes y por valles, despertando
las aves y animales y la gente:
cuál por el aire claro va volando,
cuál por el verde valle o alta cumbre   75
paciendo va segura y libremente,
cuál con el sol presente
va de nuevo al oficio,
y al usado ejercicio
do su natura o menester le inclina: 80
siempre está en llanto esta ánima mesquina,
cuando la sombra el mundo va cubriendo
o la luz se avecina.
Salid sin duelo, lágrimas, corriendo.

¿Y tú, desta mi vida ya olvidada,   85
sin mostrar un pequeño sentimiento
de que por ti Salicio triste muera,
dejas llevar, desconocida, al viento
el amor y la fe que ser guardada
eternamente sólo a mí debiera?   90
¡Oh Dios! ¿Por qué siquiera,
pues ves desde tu altura

Dying am I and nevertheless fear life;   60
I fear it with good reason, since you're leaving,
for without you living has no reason.
    I am ashamed that anyone
    should see me in this state,
    spurned by you, abandoned,   65
and now I even blush to see myself.
Do you disdain to be mistress of a soul
wherein you always dwelt and could not be
    absent for a single hour?
Flow, tears, freely; easily swiftly flow.   70

The sun unfurls and spreads its rays of light
over mountains and valleys, awakening
the birds, the animals, the human beings;
there are those that fly away through the bright air,
those that over the green valleys and the peaks   75
wander, grazing, freely and in safety;
    and those now the sun is up
    who return again to the work
    and customary pursuits
to which their nature or their needs incline them;   80
but this poor soul is always overcome
by tears, when darkness starts to cloak the world
    or light of day approaches.
Flow, tears, freely; easily swiftly flow.

And you, no longer mindful that I live,   85
nor showing even the least sign of regret
that for your sake Salicio dies of heartbreak,
throw to the winds and let them scatter all
the love and faith which rightfully should be
    dedicated eternally to me.   90
    How can it be, O God,
    when from Your vantage point

esta falsa perjura
causar la muerte de un estrecho amigo,
no recibe del cielo algún castigo?   95
Si en pago del amor yo estoy muriendo,
¿qué hará el enemigo?
Salid sin duelo, lágrimas, corriendo.

Por ti el silencio de la selva umbrosa,
por ti la esquividad y apartamiento   100
del solitario monte me agradaba;
por ti la verde hierba, el fresco viento,
el blanco lirio y colorada rosa
y dulce primavera deseaba.
¡Ay, cuánto me engañaba!   105
¡Ay, cuán diferente era
y cuán de otra manera
lo que en tu falso pecho se escondía!
Bien claro con su voz me lo decía
la siniestra corneja repitiendo   110
la desventura mía.
Salid sin duelo, lágrimas, corriendo.

¡Cuántas veces, durmiendo en la floresta,
reputándolo yo por desvarío,
vi mi mal entre sueños desdichado!   115
Soñaba que en el tiempo del estío
llevaba, por pasar allí la siesta,
a beber en el Tajo mi ganado;
y después de llegado,
sin saber de cuál arte,   120
por desusada parte
y por nuevo camino el agua se iba;
ardiendo ya con la calor estiva,
el curso, enajenado, iba siguiendo

You see this perjurer
contrive the death of so intimate a friend,
there comes to her no punishment from heaven?   95
If my love's reward is that I'm dying, what
    will an enemy deserve?
Flow, tears, freely; easily swiftly flow.

For you the silence of the shady forest
was dear to me, for you I sought the quiet   100
and seclusion of the lonely mountain,
for you I wanted the green grass and the fresh
breezes, the white lily and the pink rose,
for you I loved the sweetness of the spring.
    O, how I deceived myself!   105
    O, how it was otherwise,
    and o, how different from
what was hidden within your treacherous heart!
Was not all made clear by the sinister crow,
whose harsh voice so many times had warned me   110
    of my misfortune?
Flow, tears, freely; easily swiftly flow.

How many times, sleeping out in the fields,
when I took it for just some form of madness,
did I see my fate in a dream? Poor fool!   115
I dreamt that in the summer season I took
my flock to water in the river Tagus,
there to pass the time of the siesta,
        and when we arrived,
        (how it could be I know not)   120
        it was in a changed place
and through a new channel the water flowed.
And I was burning with summer's torrid heat,
as I pursued the new perverted course

del agua fugitiva.   125
Salid sin duelo, lágrimas, corriendo.

Tu dulce habla ¿en cúya oreja suena?
Tus claros ojos ¿a quién los volviste?
¿Por quién tan sin respeto me trocaste?
Tu quebrantada fe ¿dó la pusiste?   130
¿Cuál es el cuello que, como en cadena,
de tus hermosos brazos anudaste?
No hay corazón que baste,
aunque fuese de piedra,
viendo mi amada hiedra,   135
de mí arrancada, en otro muro asida,
y mi parra en otro olmo entretejida,
que no se esté con llanto deshaciendo
hasta acabar la vida.
Salid sin duelo, lágrimas, corriendo.   140

¿Qué no se esperará de aquí adelante,
por difícil que sea y por incierto?
O ¿qué discordia no será juntada?
y juntamente ¿qué tendrá por cierto,
o qué de hoy más no temerá el amante,   145
siendo a todo materia por ti dada?
Cuando tú enajenada
de mí, cuidado fuiste,
notable causa diste
y ejemplo a todos cuantos cubre el cielo,   150
que el más seguro tema con recelo
perder lo que estuviere poseyendo.
Salid fuera sin duelo,
salid sin duelo, lágrimas, corriendo.

Materia diste al mundo de esperanza   155
de alcanzar lo imposible y no pensado,

of that fugitive water.   125
Flow, tears, freely; easily swiftly flow.

Your sweet voice now, in whose ears does it sound?
Your bright eyes, on whom now do you turn them?
For whom so abruptly have I been exchanged?
Where have you put away your broken vows?   130
Whose neck is it that like a friendly chain
your lovely arms hold and encircle now?
    No heart could bear it, even
    if made of stone: to see
    my most beloved ivy   135
torn from me and fastened to another wall,
my vine entangled with another elm—
how can I not unmake myself in bitter
    weeping till life departs?
Flow, tears, freely; easily swiftly flow.   140

What can we not expect from this time on,
however hard or doubtful it may seem?
Or what opposites may not yet converge,
and likewise, what can the lover hold as
certain or what from today not fear,   145
since all is now made possible by you?
    When you turned your back on
    all tenderness toward me,
    what a fine excuse you gave,
to all who live on earth what an example!   150
so now the most secure may suspect, and fear
to lose all that they formerly possessed.
    Flow freely, easily:
flow, tears, freely; easily swiftly flow.

Reason you gave to all the world to hope   155
for the impossible, the unthinkable,

y de hacer juntar lo diferente,
dando a quien diste el corazón malvado,
quitándolo de mí con tal mudanza,
que siempre sonará de gente en gente.   160
La cordera paciente
con el lobo hambriento
hará su ayuntamiento,
y con las simples aves sin ruido
harán las bravas sierpes ya su nido;   165
que mayor diferencia comprehendo
de ti al que has escogido.
Salid sin duelo, lágrimas, corriendo.

Siempre de nueva leche en el verano
y en el invierno abundo ; en mi majada   170
la manteca y el queso está sobrado;
de mi cantar, pues, yo te vi agradada,
tanto, que no pudiera el mantuano
Titiro ser de ti más alabado.
No soy, pues, bien mirado,   175
tan disforme ni feo;
que aun agora me veo
en esta agua que corre clara y pura,
y cierto no trocara mi figura
con ese que de mí se está riendo;   180
¡trocara mi ventura!
Salid sin duelo, lágrimas, corriendo.

¿Cómo te vine en tanto menosprecio?
¿Cómo te fuí tan presto aborrecible?
¿Cómo te faltó en mí el conocimiento?   185
Si no tuvieras condición terrible,
siempre fuera tenido de ti en precio,
y no viera de ti este apartamiento.
¿No sabes que sin cuento

the union of what is incompatible,
when you gave your wretched heart to whom you did,
withdrawing it from me with such a change
that will forever be the talk of nations.   160
    The submissive lamb
    and the ravenous wolf
    will lie down together,
while silently, with the innocent birds
the vicious snake establishes his nest: 165
greater far is the gap I see between
    you and the one you've chosen.
Flow, tears, freely; easily swiftly flow.

Summer and winter I always have fresh milk
in plentiful supply; and from my flock   170
butter and cheese that more than meet my needs;
with my singing I saw you once so pleased
that not even Virgil, the Mantuan
Tityrus, could by you have been more praised.
    I am not, in point of fact   175
    so ugly or deformed,
    for now I view myself
in this brook which runs so clear and pure
and for sure I would not exchange my looks
with him who thinks now to have the laugh on me;   180
    my fortune, that I would change!
Flow, tears, freely; easily swiftly flow.

How did I earn from you so much contempt?
How so quickly did I become abhorrent?
Our understanding, how did it so swiftly   185
cease? But for your cruel disposition,
I should have gone on enjoying your esteem,
and never would have suffered this estrangement.
    Do you not know that I have

buscan en el estío   190
mis ovejas el frío
de la sierra de Cuenca, y el gobierno
del abrigado Estremo en el invierno?
Mas ¡qué vale el tener, si derritiendo
me estoy en llanto eterno!   195
Salid sin duelo, lágrimas, corriendo.

Con mi llorar las piedras enternecen
su natural dureza y la quebrantan,
los árboles parece que se inclinan,
las aves que me escuchan, cuando cantan,   200
con diferente voz se condolecen,
y mi morir cantando me adivinan.
Las fieras que reclinan
su cuerpo fatigado,
dejan el sosegado   205
sueño por escuchar mi llanto triste.
Tú sola contra mí te endureciste,
los ojos aun siquiera no volviendo
a los que tú heciste
salir sin duelo, lágrimas, corriendo.   210

Mas ya que a socorrer aquí no vienes,
no dejes el lugar que tanto amaste,
que bien podrás venir de mí segura.
Yo dejaré el lugar do me dejaste;
ven, si por sólo esto te detienes.   215
Ves aquí un prado lleno de verdura,
ves aquí un espesura,
ves aquí un agua clara,
en otro tiempo cara,
a quien de ti con lágrimas me quejo.   220
Quizá aquí hallarás, pues yo me alejo,

countless sheep that in summer   190
    seek the cool relief
of Cuenca's mountains and in winter seek
the pastures of sheltered Extremadura?
But what are possessions, when I'm dissolving
    in perpetual tears!   195
Flow, tears, freely; easily swiftly flow.

At the sound of my weeping, stones dissolve
their natural hardness and disintegrate;
the trees seem to bow down respectfully;
the birds that hear me, when they sing,   200
change their tune to express their sympathy
and in their song my approaching death predict;
    wild animals that rest
    their tired bodies
    abandon peaceful sleep   205
to listen to my melancholy tears;
you alone have hardened yourself against me
not even turning back to contemplate
    the tears that you have caused to
flow freely, and easily swiftly flow.   210

But, since you will not come back to save me,
do not desert this place you loved so much,
for if you come, you do not need to fear me.
I will leave this place, the place where you left me;
so come, if nothing else but that prevents you.   215
Here you can see a meadow of lush green grass,
    here you can see a wood,
    here you can see the running
    water once so dear to us,
to which I complain of you with many tears.   220
Perhaps you'll meet him here, the one who

al que todo mi bien quitarme puede;
que pues el bien le dejo,
no es mucho que el lugar también le quede.

Aquí dió fin a su cantar Salicio,   225
y sospirando en el postrero acento,
soltó de llanto una profunda vena.
Queriendo el monte al grave sentimiento
de aquel dolor en algo ser propicio,
con la pasada voz retumba y suena.   230
La blanca Filomena,
casi como dolida
y a compasión movida,
dulcemente responde al son lloroso.
Lo que cantó tras esto Nemoroso   235
decidlo vos, Piérides; que tanto
no puedo yo ni oso,
que siento enflaquecer mi débil canto.

Nemoroso
   Corrientes aguas, puras, cristalinas;
árboles que os estáis mirando en ellas,   240
verde prado de fresca sombra lleno,
aves que aquí sembráis vuestras querellas,
hiedra que por los árboles caminas,
torciendo el paso por su verde seno;
yo me vi tan ajeno   245
del grave mal que siento,
que de puro contento
con vuestra soledad me recreaba,
donde con dulce sueño reposaba,
o con el pensamiento discurría   250
por donde no hallaba
sino memorias llenas de alegría;

was able to take my happiness away,
　　which I'll bequeath to him,
so this place too may just as well be his.

Salicio here put an end to his singing,　　　　225
and, as his last syllable became a sigh,
the tears within welled up and overflowed.
In its deep bass the mountain, wishing to be
of service and to aid the expression of
such feelings of sorrow, echoes and resounds.　　230
　　Fair Philomena,
　　as if in pain herself
　　and moved to pity,
warbles a sweet reply to the doleful sound.
What Nemoroso sang next, I will let you tell,　　235
Muses, since to tell it myself I am
　　not able, nor do I dare,
for I feel my feeble voice is failing.

Nemoroso
Pure streams of crystal water blithely flowing,
trees that stand admiring your reflections,　　　240
green countryside full of refreshing shade,
birds that fill the air with your complaints,
ivy making your way up in the trees,
twisting and turning through their hearts of green:
　　so distant then my feeling　　　　　　　245
　　from the pain I suffer now
　　that in pure exultation
I rested in your solitude and rejoiced,
enjoying all the time untroubled sleep,
or in imagination running through　　　　　250
　　all the places that I knew,
which held nothing but sweet memories of joy.

y en este mismo valle, donde agora
me entristesco y me canso, en el reposo
estuve ya contento y descansado.   255
¡Oh bien caduco, vano y presuroso!
Acuérdome durmiendo aquí algún hora,
que despertando, a Elisa vi a mi lado.
¡Oh miserable hado!
¡Oh tela delicada,   260
antes de tiempo dada
a los agudos filos de la muerte!
Mas convenible fuera aquesta suerte
a los cansados años de mi vida,
que es más que el hierro fuerte,   265
pues no la ha quebrantado tu partida.

¿Dó están agora aquellos claros ojos
que llevaban tras sí, como colgada,
mi alma doquier que ellos se volvían?
¿Dó está la blanca mano delicada,   270
llena de vencimientos y despojos
que de mí mis sentidos le ofrecían?
Los cabellos que vían
con gran desprecio el oro,
como a menor tesoro,   275
¿adónde están? ¿Adónde el blando pecho?
¿Dó la coluna que el dorado techo
con presunción graciosa sostenía?
Aquesto todo agora ya se encierra,
por desventura mía,   280
en la fría, desierta y dura tierra.

¿Quién me dijera, Elisa, vida mía,
cuando en aqueste valle al fresco viento
andábamos cogiendo tiernas flores,
que había de ver con largo apartamiento   285

And in this very valley where now I
languish and feel tired even when resting,
I once was happy, rested, and at peace.   255
Oh, how fragile happiness, how vain and fleeting!
I remember here how once I fell asleep
and woke to see Elisa at my side.
    O wretched destiny!
    O insubstantial fabric,   260
    before its time surrendered
to be cut to shreds by the sharp shears of death!
How much better that fate would have suited
the weary years of my remaining life,
    more obstinate than iron,   265
since after your departure it still survives.

Where now are those bright eyes, which drew my soul
after them wheresoever they might turn,
as if it were suspended on a string?
And where is that sweet and delicate white hand,   270
clasping all the victories and the spoils
my senses willingly surrendered to it?
    The hair that I once saw,
    which was a reproach to gold
    making it seem the lesser   275
treasure, where is it now? Where the white breast?
Where is the white column, so graciously
proportioned, which upheld the golden roof?
All gone now, all of it, all entombed,
    to my eternal sorrow,   280
within the dark, the desolate, the hard earth.

Who could have known, Elisa, my love, my life,
when in this valley with the cool breeze blowing
we wandered gathering tender flowers,
that I would see, after long separation,   285

venir el triste y solitario día
que diese amargo fin a mis amores?
El cielo en mis dolores
cargó la mano tanto,
que a sempiterno llanto   290
y a triste soledad me ha condenado;
y lo que siento más es verme atado
a la pesada vida y enojosa,
solo, desamparado,
ciego sin lumbre en cárcel tenebrosa.   295

    Después que nos dejaste, nunca pace
en hartura el ganado ya, ni acude
el campo al labrador con mano llena.
No hay bien que en mal no se convierta y mude:
la mala hierba al trigo ahoga, y nace   300
en lugar suyo la infelice avena;
la tierra, que de buena
gana nos producía
flores con que solía
quitar en sólo vellas mil enojos,   305
produce agora en cambio estos abrojos,
ya de rigor de espinas intratable;
yo hago con mis ojos
crecer, lloviendo, el fruto miserable.

    Como al partir del sol la sombra crece,   310
y en cayendo su rayo se levanta
la negra escuridad que el mundo cubre,
de do viene el temor que nos espanta,
y la medrosa forma en que se ofrece
aquella que la noche nos encubre,   315
hasta que el sol descubre
su luz pura y hermosa;

that saddest and most desolate of days,
which would bring my love to such a bitter end.
    Heaven dealt me sorrows
    from such a loaded hand
    that to eternal grief   290
and lonely solitude it has condemned me;
and what afflicts me most is seeing myself
bound to a tedious and irksome life,
    alone, abandoned, blind,
locked in a gloomy prison without light.   295

Since you left us, the flock has never had
its fill, no more do the obedient fields
greet the farmers with a generous crop,
there's nothing good that does not change to ill:
weeds swamp and choke the wheat and in its place   300
accursed wild oats spring up and flourish;
    the earth, that willingly once
    provided us with flowers
    in such profusion that just
to see them could dissipate a thousand cares,   305
now produces nothing but these brambles,
intractable, owing to the harshness
    of their thorns. Tears from my eyes
rain down and help this wretched crop to grow.

As shadows lengthen when the sun goes down,   310
as, when its beams abate, a tide of darkness
rises to shroud the earth in black and brings
terrors of the night that freeze our senses,
and the horrifying forms that things assume,
when night conceals their usual shape from us,   315
    until the sun uncovers
    its pure and lovely light:

tal es la tenebrosa
noche de tu partir, en que he quedado
de sombra y de temor atormentado,   320
hasta que muerte el tiempo determine
que a ver el deseado
sol de tu clara vista me encamine.

Cual suele el ruiseñor con triste canto
quejarse, entre las hojas escondido,   325
del duro labrador, que cautamente
le despojó su caro y dulce nido
de los tiernos hijuelos, entre tanto
que del amado ramo estaba ausente,
y aquel dolor que siente   330
con diferencia tanta
por la dulce garganta
despide, y a su canto el aire suena,
y la callada noche no refrena
su lamentable oficio y sus querellas,   335
trayendo de su pena
al cielo por testigo y las estrellas;

desta manera suelto ya la rienda
a mi dolor, y así me quejo en vano
de la dureza de la muerte airada.   340
Ella en mi corazón metió la mano,
y de allí me llevó mi dulce prenda;
que aquel era su nido y su morada.
¡Ay muerte arrebatada!
Por ti me estoy quejando   345
al cielo y enojando
con importuno llanto al mundo todo:
el desigual dolor no sufre modo.
No me podrán quitar el dolorido

thus am I, in the dark night
of your absence, where I am left behind,
by shadows and uncertainty tormented   320
until the day by death has been appointed
    when I shall at last set off
to see the longed-for sun of your bright eyes.

As the nightingale, singing of heartbreak,
complains from where she's hidden in the leaves   325
of the cruel laborer who stealthily
despoiled that dear beloved nest of hers,
robbing her of her tender chicks, while she
was absent from the familiar branch,
    and the pain she feels   330
    with such rich variations
    pours so profusely forth
from her tuneful throat, that the air echoes with
her song, and the silent night does not restrain
this office of lament and accusation,   335
    as she calls on heaven
and the stars to bear witness to her pain:

just so do I give free rein to my grief,
thus do I in vain accuse the cruelty
of unrelenting death that shows no mercy;   340
it reached with its cruel hand into my heart
and took away from there my dear beloved,
for there she had her nest and dwelling-place:
    O rash precipitate death,
    you are to blame if I   345
    complain to heaven and weary
all the world with my immoderate tears!
A grief that is extreme brooks no restraint;
nothing will ever take away from me

sentir, si ya del todo   350
primero no me quitan el sentido.

   Tengo una parte aquí de tus cabellos,
Elisa, envueltos en un blanco paño,
que nunca de mi seno se me apartan;
descójolos, y de un dolor tamaño   355
enternecerme siento, que sobre ellos
nunca mis ojos de llorar se hartan.
Sin que de allí se partan,
con suspiros calientes,
más que la llama ardientes,   360
los enjugo del llanto, y de consuno
casi los paso y cuento uno a uno;
juntándolos, con un cordón los ato.
Tras esto el importuno
dolor me deja descansar un rato.   365

   Mas luego a la memoria se me ofrece
aquella noche tenebrosa, escura,
que tanto aflige esta ánima mesquina
con la memoria de mi desventura.
Verte presente agora me parece   370
en aquel duro trance de Lucina,
y aquella voz divina,
con cuyo son y acentos
a los airados vientos
pudieras amansar, que agora es muda;   375
me parece que oigo que a la cruda,
inesorable diosa demandabas
en aquel paso ayuda;
y tú, rústica diosa, ¿dónde estabas?

   ¿Íbate tanto en perseguir las fieras?   380
¿Íbate tanto en un pastor dormido?

my sense of pain, unless   350
first they take out consciousness itself.

I have here, Elisa, one lock of your hair,
which carefully I wrapped in a white cloth,
and which is never parted from my breast;
I unwrap the hair and all at once am struck   355
by such a pain that I am melted and know
my eyes will never feel they're done with weeping.
      I leave it where it is,
      and breathe on it with breath
      hotter than any flame,   360
drying with my sighs the dampness of my tears,
and almost touch and count each separate hair,
then tie it all together with a thread.
      This done, the tormenting grief
allows me just one moment of relief.   365

But then my memory is overpowered
by that dark and gloomy night which always
returns to torture this weak unhappy soul
with the memory of my ill fortune:
it seems to me I see you as you were   370
in the throes of your grim trial by Lucina;
      and that heavenly voice
      whose sound and accent
      could tame the angry winds,
and which has now forever fallen silent   375
I seem to hear again, and hear you asking
that cruel, that inexorable goddess
      for succor in your crisis.
And you, uncivil goddess, where were you then?

Was it from hunting you couldn't break away?   380
Was a sleeping shepherd too important?

143

¿Cosa pudo bastar a tal crueza,
que, comovida a compasión, oído
a los votos y lágrimas no dieras
por no ver hecha tierra tal belleza,   385
o no ver la tristeza
en que tu Nemoroso
queda, que su reposo
era seguir tu oficio, persiguiendo
las fieras por los montes, y ofreciendo   390
a tus sagradas aras los despojos?
¿Y tú, ingrata, riendo
dejas morir mi bien ante los ojos?

    Divina Elisa, pues agora el cielo
con inmortales pies pisas y mides,   395
y su mudanza ves, estando queda,
¿por qué de mí te olvidas, y no pides
que se apresure el tiempo en que este velo
rompa del cuerpo, y verme libre pueda,
y en la tercera rueda   400
contigo mano a mano
busquemos otro llano,
busquemos otros montes y otros ríos,
otros valles floridos y sombríos,
donde descanse y siempre pueda verte   405
ante los ojos míos,
sin miedo y sobresalto de perderte?—

    Nunca pusieran fin al triste lloro
los pastores, ni fueran acabadas
las canciones que sólo el monte oía,   410
si mirando las nubes coloradas,
al tramontar del sol bordadas de oro,
no vieran que era ya pasado el día.
La sombra se veía

Can anything excuse such cruelty,
that you were not moved to pity, that you paid
no heed to those vows and tears, did nothing
to prevent such beauty from becoming dust,   385
    or to prevent the despair
    to which your Nemoroso
    is condemned, whose leisure hours
were spent in following your vocation,
hunting wild animals in the mountains   390
on your holy altars to offer them?
    while you, ungrateful one,
you laughed and let her die before my eyes!

Divine Elisa, for now it is the sky
you tread and measure with immortal feet,   395
and watch its changes while remaining still,
have you forgotten me? Why do you not ask
for that time to come more quickly when this veil
of the body will be torn and I be free?
    Then in the third heaven,   400
    with you hand in hand,
    we will seek another plain,
other mountains, other flowing rivers,
other flowering shady valleys,
where I can rest forever and ever have you   405
    before my happy eyes,
without the fear and shock of losing you.

Never would those shepherds have put an end
to their sad lament, nor the songs concluded,
which none but the mountain was on hand to hear,   410
had they not realized, looking at the
colored clouds of sunset, gold-embroidered,
that the day was already past and done.
    Darkness could be seen

venir corriendo apriesa   415
ya por la falda espesa
del altísimo monte, y recordando
ambos como de sueño, y acabando
el fugitivo sol, de luz escaso,
su ganado llevando,   420
se fueron recogiendo paso a paso.

speeding ever nearer   415
   over the imposing flank
of the high mountain, and the two as if
awakening from a dream, as the fugitive
sun was dying and gave but little light,
      rounded up their sheep   420
and slowly drove them homeward to the fold.

From Egloga II
Personas: Albanio, Camila, Salicio, Nemoroso

Albanio
En medio del invierno está templada
el agua dulce desta clara fuente,
y en el verano más que nieve helada.
    ¡Oh claras ondas, cómo veo presente,
en viéndoos, la memoria de aquel día   5
de que el alma temblar y arder se siente!
    En vuestra claridad vi mi alegría
escurecerse toda y enturbiarse;
cuando os cobré perdí mi compañía.
    ¿A quién pudiera igual tormento darse,   10
que con lo que descansa otro afligido
venga mi corazón a atormentarse?
    El dulce murmurar de este ruído,
el mover de los árboles al viento,
el suave olor del prado florecido,   15
    podrían tornar, de enfermo y descontento,
cualquier pastor del mundo, alegre y sano;
yo sólo en tanto bien morir me siento.
    ¡Oh hermosura sobre el ser humano!
¡Oh claros ojos! ¡Oh cabellos de oro!   20
¡Oh cuello de marfil! ¡Oh blanca mano!
    ¿Cómo puede ora ser que en triste lloro
se convirtiese tan alegre vida,
y en tal pobreza todo mi tesoro?
    Quiero mudar lugar, y a la partida   25
quizá me dejará parte del daño
que tiene el alma casi consumida.
    ¡Cuán vano imaginar, cuán claro engaño

148

From Eclogue II
Personae: Albanio, Camila, Salicio, Nemoroso

Albanio
    Even in the depths of winter, the water
of this clear spring is mild and sweet, while in
the summer, snow itself's not cooler.
    O limpid stream, how clearly when I look in
your water I see in memory the day   5
that has my soul still shivering and burning!
    In your transparency I saw my joy
become all muddied and confused; when I
next saw you I lost my true companion.
    Who ever suffered such bitterness as I,   10
when that from which another would take comfort
to my poor heart brings only misery?
    This sweet sound of water, its soft murmur,
the wind in the trees, their branches swaying,
the gentle perfume of the flowery meadow,   15
    could change the state of any sad and ailing
shepherd, revive his spirits, make him healthy.
Amid such blessings I alone am dying.
    O awesome, rare and superhuman beauty!
O shining eyes, o lovely, golden curls,   20
o white, white hand, o neck of ivory!
    How can it be such happiness now turns
into such sadness and such bitter tears
and all my treasure into worthless dust?
    I think of going away, perhaps my cares   25
may be avoided by a change of scene,
before they've finally eaten up my soul.
    What a delusion, how obviously vain

es darme yo a entender que con partirme,
de mí se ha de partir un mal tamaño!   30
¡Ay miembros fatigados, y cuán firme
es el dolor que os cansa y enflaquece!
¡Oh si pudiese un rato aquí dormirme!
Al que velando el bien nunca se ofrece,
quizá que el sueño le dará durmiendo   35
algún placer, que presto desfallece
en tus manos ¡oh sueño! me encomiendo.

Salicio
    ¡Cuán bienaventurado
aquel puede llamarse
que con la dulce soledad se abraza,   40
y vive descuidado,
y lejos de empacharse
en lo que al alma impide y embaraza!
No ve la llena plaza,
ni la soberbia puerta   45
de los grandes señores,
ni los aduladores
a quien la hambre del favor despierta;
no le será forzoso
rogar, fingir, temer y estar quejoso.   50

    A la sombra holgando
de un alto pino o robre,
o de alguna robusta y verde encina,
el ganado contando
de su manada pobre;   55
que por la verde selva se avecina,
plata cendrada y fina,
oro luciente y puro,
baja y vil le parece,
y tanto lo aborrece,   60

to suppose that somehow by departing
I can be quit of such outstanding pain!   30
    O tired limbs, how immovable and deep
the grief that wearies and enfeebles you.
If only for a moment I could sleep!
    To him who waking finds no happiness
sleep perhaps can give until he wakes   35
some pleasure, though it quickly vanishes.
Into your hands I commend myself, o sleep!

Salicio
    How happy, we may say
is the simple man, he
who devotes himself to sweet solitude,   40
and chases cares away,
never content to be
with things that bind and vex the soul embroiled.
He does not see the crowd
in the square, the emblazoned door   45
of the haughty nobleman
nor the flatterers of whom
thirst for favor awakens ever more.
He has no call to
beg, dissemble, fear or curse his fortune.   50

    Resting in the agreeable
shade of some tall pine or oak
or stretched beneath the ilex's green crown,
counting the individuals
of his scant flock   55
as they congregate around him on the down,
he knows that silver's shine
or gold's seductive glitter
are vile and worthless to him,
and so abhors them   60

que aun no piensa que dello está seguro;
y como está en su seso,
rehuye la cerviz del grave peso.

　　Convida a dulce sueño
aquel manso ruído   65
del agua que la clara fuente envía,
y las aves sin dueño
con canto no aprendido
hinchen el aire de dulce armonía;
háceles compañía,   70
a la sombra volando,
y entre varios olores
gustando tiernas flores,
la solícita abeja susurrando;
los árboles y el viento   75
al sueño ayudan con su movimiento.

　　¿Quién duerme aquí? ¿Dó está que no le veo?
¡Oh! helo allí. Dichoso tú, que aflojas
la cuerda al pensamiento o al deseo.
　　¡Oh natura, cuán pocas obras cojas   80
en el mundo son hechas por tu mano!
Creciendo el bien, menguando las congojas,
　　el sueño diste al corazón humano
para que al despertar más se alegrase
del estado gozoso, alegre y sano;   85
　　que, como si de nuevo le hallase,
hace aquel intervalo que ha pasado
que el nuevo gusto nunca al fin se pase.
　　Y al que de pensamiento fatigado
el sueño baña con licor piadoso,   90
curando el corazón despedazado,
　　aquel breve descanso, aquel reposo
basta para cobrar de nuevo aliento,

merely to think of them can make him shudder,
and being of sound mind,
he vows to keep his neck free from their burden.

   To a delightful sleep
the soft sound of running   65
water from the limpid stream invites;
and the unstudied song
of the ungoverned birds
fills the air with musical delights,
to the accompaniment—   70
wandering in the shade,
among perfumed bowers,
sipping tender flowers—
of the busy bee humming in the glade;
sleep is aided by the breeze   75
gently rocking the branches of the trees.

   Someone's sleeping here? Where is he, why can't I
see him? Ah, there he is! Lucky you, who can
let go of all your thoughts or your desires.
   O nature, how few among the things you make   80
for this world of ours come halting from your hand!
For the increase of good, and mitigation
   of sorrow, you gave sleep to the human heart
in order that on waking it should the more
rejoice in the pleasures of its healthy state,   85
   with a joy like something new, not known before;
in this way the short interval that passed
ensures that pleasure does not lose its savor.
   As for the man with weary troubled thought,
sleep bathes him in its merciful waters   90
and heals the fractures of a broken heart;
   that brief interlude, that period of rest
gives him time to breathe and find new energy

con que se pase el curso trabajoso.
Llegarme quiero cerca con buen tiento,   95
y ver, si de mí fuere conocido,
si es del número triste o del contento.

Albanio es este que está aquí dormido,
o yo conozco mal. Albanio es, cierto.
Duerme, garzón cansado y afligido.   100
¡Por cuán mejor librado tengo un muerto
que acaba el curso de la vida humana
y es reducido a más seguro puerto,
que el que, viviendo acá, de vida ufana
y de estado gozoso, noble y alto,   105
es derrocado de fortuna insana!
Dicen que este mancebo dió un gran salto:
que de amorosos bienes fué abundante,
y agora es pobre, miserable y falto.
No sé la historia bien; mas quien delante   110
se halló al duelo me contó algún poco
del grave caso deste pobre amante.

Albanio
¿Es esto sueño, o ciertamente toco
la blanca mano? ¡Ah sueño! ¿estás burlando!
Yo estábate creyendo como loco.   115
¡Oh cuitado de mí! Tú vas volando
con prestas alas por la ebúrnea puerta;
yo quédome tendido aquí llorando.
¿No basta el grave mal en que despierta
el alma vive, o por mejor decillo,   120
está muriendo de una vida incierta?

Salicio
Albanio, deja el llanto, que en oíllo
me aflijo.

with which to face the troubles that assail him.
    I will approach carefully, with discretion,   95
to see, supposing it's someone that I know,
which group he's of, the sad or the contented.

    This person sleeping here is Albanio, if
I'm not mistaken. Albanio it is,
for sure. Sleep on, weary and afflicted one.   100
    How much better off, I'd say, is the dead man,
the one who, reaching the end of human life,
is at last conducted to a safe haven,
    compared with him on earth, who at the height
of his happiness, prosperity and pride   105
is felled by just one stroke of crazy fortune!
    This young man, they say, experienced a great
fall; once richly provided with love's favors
he now is poor, grief-stricken, destitute.
    I am not fully acquainted with the story,   110
but one who was witness to the sad event
told me of this poor lover's grievous case.

Albanio
    Is it a dream, or am I really touching
that white hand? Ah, dream, do you mock me then?
I was like a madman, thinking you were real.   115
    O wretched me, now you are gone, sailing
off on swift wings through the ivory gate,
while I am left here prostrate and lamenting.
    Is it not enough, the desperate state
in which the soul lives while awake, or rather,   120
in which it's dying of an uncertain life?

Salicio
    Albanio, cease your weeping, for it pains me
to hear it.

Albanio
¿Quién presente está a mi duelo?

Salicio
Aquí está quien te ayudará a sentillo.

Albanio
  ¿Aquí estás tú, Salicio? Gran consuelo   125
me fuera en cualquier mal tu compañía;
mas tengo en esto por contrario al cielo.

Salicio
  Parte de tu trabajo ya me había
contado Galafrón, que fué presente
en aqueste lugar el mismo día;   130
  mas no supo decir del acidente
la causa principal; bien que pensaba
que era mal que decir no se consiente;
  y a la sazón en la ciudad yo estaba,
como tú sabes bien, aparejando   135
aquel largo camino que esperaba;
  y esto que digo me contaron cuando
torné a volver; mas yo te ruego agora,
si esto no es enojoso que demando,
  que particularmente el punto y hora,   140
la causa, el daño cuentes y el proceso;
que el mal comunicado se mejora.

Albanio
  Con un amigo tal verdad es eso,
cuando el mal sufre cura, mi Salicio;
mas éste ha penetrado hasta el hueso.   145
  Verdad es que la vida y ejercicio
común, y el amistad que a ti me ayunta,
mandan que complacerte sea mi oficio;

Albanio
Who is present at my grief?

Salicio
One who if he can will help you bear it.

Albanio
Is it you, Salicio? Your company   125
would console me in most kinds of crisis,
but in the present case my opponent's heaven.

Salicio
Something of your troubles, Galafrón
has already told me, he was present
in this same place the day it all began   130
but could not say what was the chief cause
of your misfortune, though he imagined
it was some ill that could not well be told;
and as you know, I at the time was in
the city, making preparations for that   135
long journey I was obliged to go on;
this business we speak of, well, it's something
I heard about on my return, but now,
I beg you, tell, if it is not too painful,
of this affair the melancholy details: 140
when exactly, where and how did it occur?
Tell me all, for misfortune shared grows lighter.

Albanio
Certainly, if one's troubles have a cure,
Salicio, a friend like you can help;
but this is a wound that's cut me to the bone.   145
It's true that our shared life and occupation
and friendship's ties that bind us both together
oblige me in all things to satisfy you;

mas ¿qué haré? que el alma ya barrunta,
que quiero renovar en la memoria   150
la herida mortal de aguda punta;
　　y póneme delante aquella gloria
pasada, y la presente desventura,
para espantarme de la horrible historia.
　　Por otra parte, pienso que es cordura   155
renovar tanto el mal que me atormenta,
que a morir venga de tristeza pura.
　　Y por esto, Salicio, entera cuenta
te daré de mi mal como pudiere,
aunque el alma rehuya y no consienta.   160
　　Quise bien, y querré mientras rigiere
aquestos miembros el espirtu mío,
aquella por quien muero, si muriere.
　　En este amor no entré por desvarío,
ni lo traté, como otros, con engaños,   165
ni fué por eleción de mi albedrío.
　　Desde mis tiernos y primeros años
a aquella parte me inclinó mi estrella,
y a aquel fiero destino de mis daños.
　　Tú conociste bien una doncella,   170
de mi sangre y abuelos descendida,
más que la misma hermosura bella.
　　En su verde niñez, siendo ofrecida
por montes y por selvas a Diana,
ejercitaba allí su edad florida.   175
　　Yo, que desde la noche á la mañana
y del un sol al otro, sin cansarme,
seguía la caza con estudio y gana,
　　por deudo y ejercicio a conformarme
vine con ella en tal domestiqueza,   180
que della un punto no sabía apartarme.
　　Iba de un hora en otra la estrecheza
haciéndose mayor, acompañada

but what can I do? my anxious soul suspects
that I'm about to revive the memory   150
of a fatal wound, dealt by a sharp arrow,
   and lays before me those past days of glory
side by side with my present lack of fortune,
warning me not to retell the fearful story.
   On the other hand, it may be opportune   155
so to dwell on the trouble that torments me
that grief alone will bring about my death.
   Therefore, Salicio, I'll give you as complete
an account of my illness as I'm able,
however much my soul may shrink from it.   160
   I loved, and I know that love I always will,
so long as my spirit governs these my limbs,
the one for whom I'll die, if die I must.
   It was no madness that led me to this love,
nor did I seek it, as others do, with guile   165
nor yet did I choose it of my own free will:
   from my earliest, tenderest years it was
my ill star inclined me in that direction,
the way of my cruel and fatal destiny.
   You've met her and you know her well, that maiden,   170
descended from my same blood and lineage,
with a face that's lovelier than beauty's own:
   since earliest days she had been a devotee
of Diana, in the mountains and the woods,
and there she passed the prime days of her youth.   175
   I, from night till morning, from one day's sunrise
till the next, was with her, and tirelessly
followed the hunt with diligence and zeal;
   through kinship and through habit I became
so accustomed to her presence, so familiar,   180
I could not be away from her a moment.
   All the time our intimacy grew more
and more complete and together with it grew

de un amor sano y lleno de pureza.
¿Qué montaña dejó de ser pisada   185
de nuestros pies? ¿Qué bosque o selva umbrosa
no fué de nuestra caza fatigada?

Albanio
    Aconteció que en una ardiente siesta,   431
viniendo de la caza fatigados,
en el mejor lugar desta floresta,
    que es este donde estamos asentados,
a la sombra de un árbol aflojamos   435
las cuerdas a los arcos trabajados.
    En aquel prado allí nos reclinamos,
y del céfiro fresco recogiendo
el agradable espirtu, respiramos.
    Las flores, a los ojos ofreciendo   440
diversidad estraña de pintura,
diversamente así estaban oliendo.
    Y en medio aquesta fuente clara y pura,
que como de cristal resplandecía,
mostrando abiertamente su hondura,   445
    el arena, que de oro parecía,
de blancas pedrezuelas variada,

a healthy love that was entirely pure.
No mountain did our feet omit to tread,   185
no wood was there, no shady forest whose
stillness was not troubled by our hunting.

Albanio goes on to describe how they spent their days together, the
different animals and birds they hunted and the methods they used.
After telling how on his part friendship turned into passionate love,
he breaks off, saying it would not be right to reveal more of his feel-
ings. Presumably he has in mind the old troubadour tradition that
love should be kept secret. Salicio remonstrates with him and speaks
of the danger of allowing yourself to be ruled by love: "Who would
be so unnatural as to give / an enemy the keys to all his wealth / and
put himself into someone else's hands?" (lines 386–88). Eventually
Albanio agrees to continue his account, on condition that when he
finishes he is left alone.

Albanio
It happened that one burning hot siesta,   431
after returning weary from the chase,
in this countryside's most perfect spot,
    that is to say, right here where we are sitting,
we sought the refuge of a shady tree   435
and released the tension of our tight-strung bows;
    over there on the grass we took our ease,
lying full length, recovering our breath
with the assistance of the refreshing breeze.
    The flowers offered an extraordinary   440
diversity of colors to the eye
and an equal variety of scents,
    and in the middle of it all this spring,
so clear and pure, glittered like crystal,
so transparent that you could see the bottom;   445
    the sand, which might have been grains of purest gold
was embellished with white pebbles, in places

por do manaba el agua, se bullía.
En derredor ni sola una pisada
de fiera o de pastor o de ganado   450
a la sazón estaba señalada.
    Después que con el agua resfriado
hubimos el calor, y juntamente
la sed de todo punto mitigado,
        ella, que con cuidado diligente   455
a conocer mi mal tenía el intento,
y a escudriñar el ánimo doliente,
        con nuevo ruego y firme juramento
me conjuró y rogó que le contase
la causa de mi grave pensamiento;   460
        y si era amor, que no me recelase
de hacelle mi caso manifiesto,
y demostralle aquella que yo amase,
        que me juraba que también en esto
el verdadero amor que me tenía   465
con pura voluntad estaba presto.
    Yo, que tanto callar ya no podía,
y claro descubrir menos osaba
lo que en el alma triste se sentía,
        le dije que en aquella fuente clara   470
vería de aquella que yo tanto amaba
abiertamente la hermosa cara.
    Ella, que ver aquésta deseaba,
con menos diligencia discurriendo
de aquella con que el paso apresuraba,   475
        a la pura fontana fué corriendo,
y en viendo el agua, toda fué alterada,
en ella su figura sola viendo.
    Y no de otra manera, arrebatada,
del agua rehuyó, que si estuviera   480
de la rabiosa enfermedad tocada.

where the water ran rippling and bubbling.
All around no footprint, nor any other
sign of living thing, nor beast nor shepherd,   450
was anywhere at that moment to be seen.
  After we had with water from the spring
both refreshed ourselves, and at the same time
fully quenched our thirst, she turned to me,
    solicitous and bent on finding out   455
the exact nature of my problem and
the reason why my soul was sunk in grief;
    with renewed pleas and solemn promises
she conjured me, begging me to tell her
the reason for my melancholy thoughts,   460
    and said that if it was love I should not fear
to tell her all about it, everything,
and even to point out the one I loved;
    for she swore to me that in this matter
the true pure love she entertained for me   465
was with the best intentions at my service.
  I, finding myself unable to keep quiet
and daring even less reveal the truth
about the feelings that burdened my sad heart,
    told her if she looked in that limpid spring   470
she would see in perfect clarity displayed
the lovely countenance of her I loved.
  She, curious to know precisely this,
did not stop to think: her understanding
could not keep pace with the speed at which she leapt   475
    to her feet, rushed to the pure spring and looked
in its clear water. And as she looked, her face
changed, for her face, her own face, was all she saw;
    and from the water she recoiled and fled
as hurriedly as if she were infected   480
with the mad rage of hydrophobia;

Y sin mirarme, desdeñosa y fiera,
no sé qué allá entre dientes murmurando,
me dejó aquí, y aquí quiere que muera.

Albanio
     Si mi turbada vista no me miente.   766
paréceme que vi entre rama y rama
una ninfa llegar a aquella fuente.
     Quiero llegar allá; quizá, si ella ama,
me dirá alguna cosa con que engañe   770
con algún falso alivio aquesta llama.
     Y no se me da nada que desbañe
mi alma, si es contrario a lo que creo;
que a quien no espera bien no hay mal que dañe.
     ¡Oh santos dioses! ¿Qué es esto que veo?   775
¿Es error de fantasma convertida
en forma de mi amor y mi deseo?
     Camila es esta que está aquí dormida;
no puede de otra ser su hermosura;
la razón está clara y conocida: 780
     una obra sola quiso la natura
hacer como ésta, y rompió luego apriesa
la estampa do fué hecha tal figura.
     ¿Quién podrá luego de su forma espresa
el traslado sacar, si la maestra   785
misma no basta, y ella lo confiesa?
     Mas ya que es cierto el bien que a mí se muestra
¿cómo podré llegar a despertalla,
temiendo yo la luz que a ella me adiestra?
     ¿Si solamente de poder tocalla   790

affording me no look, indignant, proud,
and muttering who knows what between her teeth,
she left me here. And here she would have me die.

Albanio continues to describe his grief. Eventually Salicio leaves
Albanio alone as he promised he would, and Camilla arrives on the
scene, pursuing a wounded deer she has shot. Deciding to postpone
the chase, she lies down to sleep. Albanio finds her.

Albanio
  If my troubled sight does not deceive me,   766
I think I saw, moving behind the branches,
a nymph, who seemed to be heading for that spring.
  Let me go closer, maybe if she loves,
she can teach me some lover's trick with which   770
to bring to this burning flame some false relief.
  And I need have no fear of being upset
if it isn't what I want, since nothing
can disappoint him who for nothing hopes.
  O, holy gods! What have we here? Is this   775
some deceiving phantom that has adopted
the likeness of my love and my desire?
  No, it is Camilla, and she is asleep;
such beauty cannot belong to any other.
The fact is obvious and admits no question: 780
  when Nature decided on this masterwork
she made but the one model and then
she quickly broke the mold in which the figure
  had been formed. Who can make a true copy
of the original if the artist   785
herself is unable to and confesses it?
  But now I am quite certain of my good
fortune, how will I ever dare to wake her,
when I fear the very light that leads me to her?
  Perhaps if I can bring myself to touch her   790

perdiese el miedo yo? Mas ¿si despierta?…
Si despierta, tenella y no soltalla.
Esta osadía temo que no es cierta.
Mas ¿qué me puede hacer? Quiero llegarme.
En fin, ella está agora como muerta.   795
    Cabe ella por lo menos asentarme
bien puedo; mas no ya como solía.
¡Oh mano poderosa de matarme!
¿Viste cuánto tu fuerza en mí podía?
¿Por qué para sanarme no la pruebas?   800
Que tu poder a todo bastaría.

Camila
    Socórreme, Diana.

Albanio
    No te muevas,
que no te he de soltar; escucha un poco.

Camila
    ¿Quién me dijera, Albanio, tales nuevas?
    Ninfas del verde bosque á vos invoco,   805
a vos pido socorro desta fuerza.
¿Qué es esto, Albanio? Dime si estás loco.

Albanio
    Locura debe ser la que me fuerza
a querer más que el alma y que la vida
a la que a aborrecerme así se esfuerza.   810

Camila
    Yo debo ser de ti la aborrecida,
pues me quieres tratar de tal manera,
siendo tuya la culpa conocida.

that fear will go away . . . but if she wakes?
If she wakes, I must seize her and not let go.
    Such daring, though, is only an illusion.
And yet, what harm can she do me? I will approach;
after all, it's only as if she were dead.   795
    I can at least sit down here beside her
But now it cannot be as once it was.
O hand, you have it in your power to kill me!
    Have you not seen what you can do to me?
Why can you not use that power to heal me?   800
It has the strength to do anything at all.

Camila
    Diana! Help!

Albanio
    Be still, don't try to struggle,
I don't intend to let you go. Just listen!

Camila
Whoever heard of such a thing, Albanio!
    Nymphs of the green woods, I call on you to help,   805
I implore your aid against this violation!
What does this mean, Albanio? Are you mad?

Albanio
    It must be madness, since it forces me
to love more than my soul, more than my life,
one with such a strong resolve to hate me.   810

Camila
    I must be the one who's hated by *you*,
seeing you wish to treat me in this way,
when your sin against me's plain for all to see.

Albanio
    ¿Yo culpa contra ti? Si la primera
no está por cometer, Camila mía,   815
en tu desgracia y disfavor yo muera.

Camila
    ¿Tú no violaste nuestra compañía,
queriéndola torcer por el camino
que de la vida honesta se desvía?

Albanio
    ¿Cómo de sola un hora el desatino   820
ha de perder mil años de servicio,
si el arrepentimiento tras él vino?

Camila
    Aqueste es de los hombres el oficio:
tentar el mal, y si es malo el suceso,
pedir con humildad perdón del vicio.   825

Albanio
    ¿Qué tenté yo, Camila?

Camila
    Bueno es eso.
Esta fuente lo diga, que ha quedado
por un testigo de tu mal proceso.

Albanio
    Si puede ser mi yerro castigado
con muerte, con deshonra o con tormento,   830
vesme aquí, estoy a todo aparejado.

Albanio
   I sin against you? If ever I have sinned
against you, Camilla dearest, may I   815
forever suffer your hatred and contempt!

Camila
   Did you not violate our friendship, when
you tried to take it down the crooked path
that leads away from chastity and honor?

Albanio
   You mean to say a single moment's folly   820
can cancel out a thousand years of service,
though repentance followed rapidly behind?

Camila
   This is ever the way of men, to attempt
an evil act, and when it turns out badly
humbly to implore pardon for their sin.   825

Albanio
   What sin is mine, Camilla?

Camila
   Oh, wonderful!
Why not ask this spring, which was here at the time,
a witness to your wicked undertaking?

Albanio
   If for my fault you think I deserve to be punished
with death or with dishonor or to be tortured,   830
here you have me, ready to take what comes.

Camila
  Suéltame ya la mano, que el aliento
  me falta de congoja.

Albanio
  He muy gran miedo
  que te me irás, que corres más que el viento.

Camila
  No estoy como solía, que no puedo   835
  moverme ya, de mal ejercitada.
  Suelta, que casi me has quebrado un dedo.

Albanio
  ¿Estarás, si te suelto, sosegada,
  mientras con razón clara yo te muestro
  que fuiste sin razón de mí enojada?   840

Camila
  Eres tú de razones gran maestro.
  Suelta, que sí estaré.

Albanio
  Primero jura
  por la primera fe del amor nuestro.

Camila
  Yo juro por la ley sincera y pura
  de la amistad pasada, de sentarme,   845
  y de escuchar tus quejas muy segura.
  ¡Cuál me tienes la mano, de apretarme
  con esa dura mano, descreído!

Albanio
  ¡Cuál me tienes el alma de dejarme!

Camila
    Let go of me, I can scarcely breathe, I'm so
upset.

Albanio
    I'm afraid that if I let go
you'll escape; you can run like the wind, I know.

Camila
    Not any longer. I can scarcely move,   835
after the wretched way I have been used.
Let go, you've almost broken my finger.

Albanio
    If I let you go, will you promise to be still,
while I prove to you with simple reasoning
that you'd no reason to be angry with me?   840

Camila
    Who are you to talk of reason? All right,
let go of me, I promise to stay.

Albanio
    Swear first
swear on the honor of our childhood love.

Camila
    I swear by all the pure and honest laws
of our past friendship that I will quietly sit   845
and listen obediently to your complaints.
    Look what you've done to my hand, you barbarian
by crushing it in those rough hands of yours!

Albanio
Look what you've done to my heart by leaving me!

Camila

Mi prendedero de oro ¡si es perdido!...   850
¡Oh cuitada de mí! Mi prendedero
desde aquel valle aquí se me ha caído.

Albanio

Mira no se cayese allá primero,
antes de aqueste al Val de la Hortiga.

Camila

Doquier que se perdió, buscallo quiero.   855

Albanio

Yo iré a buscallo, escusa esa fatiga;
que no puedo sufrir que aquesta arena
abrase el blanco pie de mi enemiga.

Camila

Pues que quieres tomar por mí esta pena,
derecho ve primero a aquellas hayas;   860
que allí estuve yo echada un hora buena.

Albanio

Ya voy; mas entre tanto no te vayas.

Camila

Seguro vé, que antes verás mi muerte
que tú me cobres ni a tus manos hayas.

Albanio

¡Ah, ninfa desleal! Y ¿desa suerte   865
se guarda el juramento que me diste?

Camila

    My gold pin! Oh dear, oh dear, it's disappeared   850
I've lost my golden pin, I must have dropped it
on my way here from the other valley!

Albanio

    Are you sure you didn't lose it before that,
back in the place they call the Vale of Nettles?

Camila

Wherever it was, I have to go and find it.   855

Albanio

    I'll go look for it. Don't you go yourself,
how can I permit this burning sand
to scald the white foot of my sweet enemy.

Camila

    Well, since you're kind enough to do this for me,
go and look first under that clump of beech trees;   860
I lay there resting for an hour or more.

Albanio

    All right, but promise to stay here while I'm gone.

Camila

Off you go, then. . . . And now, be sure you'll see me
dead before I'm in your clutches again!

Albanio

    O treacherous girl! Is this the way you keep
the solemn oath your swore to me just now?   865

*While Albanio in a soliloquy wishes he were dead, Salicio and Nem-
oroso appear and listen to his talk of dying to end his troubles.*

Salicio
Escucha, que algún mal hacerse quiere,   883
o cierto tiene trastornado el seso.

Albanio
Aquí tuviese yo quien mal me quiere.   885
Descargado me siento de un gran peso;
paréceme que vuelo, despreciando
monte, choza, ganado, leche y queso.
¿No son aquestos pies? Con ellos ando.
Ya caigo en ello, el cuerpo se me ha ido;   890
sólo el espirtu es este que hora mando.
¿Hale hurtado alguno o escondido
mientras mirando estaba yo otra cosa?
¿O si quedó por caso allí dormido?
Una figura de color de rosa   895
estaba allí durmiendo; ¿si es aquélla
mi cuerpo? No, que aquélla es muy hermosa

Nemoroso
Gentil cabeza; no daría por ella
yo para mi traer sólo un cornado.

Albanio
¿A quién iré del hurto a dar querella?   900

Salicio
Estraño ejemplo es ver en qué ha parado
este gentil mancebo, Nemoroso;
¡Y a nosotros que le hemos más tratado,
    manso, cuerdo, agradable, virtuoso,
sufrido, conversable, buen amigo,   905
y con un alto ingenio, gran reposo!

Salicio
　　Listen, he intends to do himself some harm.　　883
It's driven him mad, for sure, his mind is gone!

Albanio
If only I had some enemy to fight!　　885
　　I feel as if I've shaken off some great
burden, as if I'm floating, looking down
on hills and huts, on cattle, milk and cheese.
　　Are these not feet? They're what I use for walking.
I've got it now. My body's disappeared;　　890
the spirit only now is in control.
　　Did someone steal it, did someone hide it,
while I wasn't looking? Or did I perhaps
leave it behind while it was sleeping? I did
　　see a figure there, asleep, rose-colored,　　895
was that it? Could that have been my body?
No, that one was beautiful, so beautiful!

Nemoroso
　　Poor head! It's absolutely worthless, I'd give
nothing for it now, not a single cent!

Albanio
Where can I report the theft? Whom can I sue?　　900

Salicio
　　What a remarkable thing it is to see
what's happened to this fine young man, Nemoroso,
who when he was with us, his best friends, was
　　mild and sensible, so good, so pleasant,
patient and such good company, such a　　905
faithful friend, intelligent and modest too.

Albanio
   Yo podré poco, o hallaré testigo
de quién hurtó mi cuerpo; aunque esté ausente,
yo lo perseguiré como enemigo.
   ¿Sabrásme decir dél, mi clara fuente?   910
Dímelo, si lo sabes; así Febo
nunca tus frescas ondas escaliente.
   Allá dentro en lo fondo está un mancebo
de laurel coronado, y en la mano
un palo propio, como yo, de acebo.   915
   Hola, ¿quién está allá? Responde, hermano.
¡Válgame Dios! O tu eres sordo o mudo,
o enemigo mortal del trato humano.
   Espirtu soy, de carne ya desnudo,
que busco el cuerpo mío, que me ha hurtado   920
algún ladrón malvado, injusto y crudo.
   Callar que callarás. ¿Hasme escuchado?
¡Oh santo Dios! Mi cuerpo mismo veo,
o yo tengo el sentido trastornado.
   ¡Oh cuerpo! Hete hallado, y no lo creo;   925
tanto sin ti me hallo descontento.
Pon fin ya a tu destierro y mi deseo.

Nemoroso
   Sospecho que el contino pensamiento
que tuvo de morir antes de agora
le representa aqueste apartamiento.   930

Salicio
   Como del que velando siempre llora,
quedan durmiendo las especies llenas
del dolor que en el alma triste mora.

Albanio

I'll find witnesses, so help me God, I'll know
who stole my body! Wherever he is
I'll track him down, like a mortal enemy!
    Can you tell me who he is, you crystal spring?   910
If you know him, tell me, and I'll pray
that Phoebus never overheats your waters.
    But look, under the water there's someone,
a young man crowned with laurel, with a stick
in his hand, just like mine, a holly bough.   915
    Hallo there, who are you? Answer me brother!
God help us, are you deaf and dumb? Or have you
sworn forever to forgo human converse?
    I am a spirit, of all my flesh stripped bare,
I'm looking for my body, which was stolen   920
by some vile thief, some wicked heartless knave.
    Nothing to say? Have you even heard me?
God Almighty! That is my own body
I am seeing, or else I have gone mad.
    O body, I've found you, I can't believe it!   925
Please, I'm so unhappy without you, return
from your exile and answer my desire!

Nemoroso

    I fear the continual thought of death
he has been entertaining has given him
this sense of separation from himself.   930

Salicio

    If a man is always weeping when awake,
his sleeping mind will be filled with images
of the pain that in his sad soul always dwells.

Albanio
Si no estás en cadenas, sal ya fuera
a darme verdadera forma de hombre,   935
que agora sólo el nombre me ha quedado.
Y si no estás forzado en ese suelo,
dímelo; que si al cielo que me oyere,
con quejas no moviere y llanto tierno,
convocaré el infierno y reino escuro,   940
y romperé su muro de diamante,
como hizo el amante blandamente
por la consorte ausente, que cantando
estuvo halagando las culebras
de las hermanas negras mal peinadas.   945

Nemoroso
¡De cuán desvariadas opiniones
saca buenas razones el cuitado!

Salicio
El curso acostumbrado del ingenio,
aunque le falte el genio que lo mueva,
con la fuga que lleva, corre un poco;   950
y aunque éste está hora loco, no por eso
ha de dar al travieso su sentido
en todo, habiendo sido cual tú sabes.

Albanio
If you are not in chains, reveal yourself, come
forth and give me back the true form of a man,   935
at present only the name remains to me;
and if you are imprisoned there below
tell me, for if heaven's not moved to listen
by my complaints and by my tender weeping,
I will call on hell and the dark regions   940
and batter down their adamantine wall,
like the famous lover, that time he went
to rescue his missing consort, and used
his sweet song to cajole the black sisters,
beguiling the snakes in their dishevelled hair.   945

Nemoroso
What reasonable conclusions he produces,
poor devil, from such unreasonable thoughts!

Salicio
The mind's accustomed movement, even when
it lacks the vital spirit that directs it,
runs on a little while under its own   950
momentum, and even though the fellow's mad
you can't say he's entirely lost to reason,
especially when you think how he once was.

*Salicio and Nemoroso, seeing that Albanio is on the point of em-
bracing the figure in the water and drowning himself, subdue him
by force. When he is a little calmer, Nemoroso speaks of a wise man
living in the region of Alba de Tormes, who might be able to help. This
leads on to a history of the family of the Dukes of Alba, which lasts
for another eight hundred lines or so.*

Egloga III
Personas: Tirreno, Alcino

Aquella voluntad honesta y pura,
ilustre y hermosísima María,
que en mí de celebrar tu hermosura,
tu ingenio y tu valor estar solía,
a despecho y pesar de la ventura   5
que por otro camino me desvía,
está y estará en mí tanto clavada,
cuanto del cuerpo el alma acompañada.

Y aun no se me figura que me toca
aqueste oficio solamente en vida;   10
mas con la lengua muerta y fría en la boca
pienso mover la voz a ti debida.
Libre mi alma de su estrecha roca,
por el Estigio lago conducida,
celebrándote irá, y aquel sonido   15
hará parar las aguas del olvido.

Mas la fortuna, de mi mal no harta,
me aflige y de un trabajo en otro lleva;
ya de la patria, ya del bien me aparta,
ya mi paciencia en mil maneras prueba;   20
y lo que siento más, es que la carta,
donde mi pluma en tu alabanza mueva,
poniendo en su lugar cuidados vanos,
me quita y me arrebata de las manos.

Pero, por más que en mí su fuerza pruebe,   25
no tornará mi corazón mudable;

Eclogue III
Personae: Tirreno, Alcino

That pure and honorable sense of duty,
illustrious and most beautiful Maria,
I have had to celebrate your beauty,
your wit and intelligence and your rare
quality, despite the adverse destiny   5
that forces me to turn my steps elsewhere,
will always be in me as firmly fixed
as the body and the soul are intermixed.

Nor do I see it as only during life
that it falls to me to perform this office,   10
for with the tongue cold and dead in my mouth
I aim to raise the voice I owe to you,
and my soul, when freed from its narrow prison
and ferried over the waters of the Styx,
will sing of you, and the sound it gives out then   15
will turn back the flood tide of oblivion.

But fortune, never tired of doing me harm
assails me and imposes endless labors,
dividing me from happiness or home,
or testing my patience in a thousand ways;   20
and what troubles me most is that the page
my pen ought to be filling with your praise
it snatches from my hand and rips and tears,
replacing it with unprofitable cares.

But however much it tries with force to rule me   25
it will not make my faithful heart inconstant;

nunca dirán jamás que me remueve
fortuna de un estudio tan loable.
Apolo y las hermanas, todas nueve,
me darán ocio y lengua con que hable   30
lo menos de lo que en tu ser cupiere,
que esto será lo más que yo pudiere.

En tanto no te ofenda ni te harte
tratar del campo y soledad que amaste,
ni desdeñes aquesta inculta parte   35
de mi estilo, que en algo ya estimaste.
Entre las armas del sangriento Marte,
do apenas hay quien su furor contraste,
hurté de el tiempo aquesta breve suma,
tomando, ora la espada, ora la pluma.   40

Aplica, pues, un rato los sentidos
al bajo són de mi zampoña ruda,
indina de llegar a tus oídos,
pues de ornamento y gracia va desnuda;
mas a las veces son mejor oídos   45
el puro ingenio y lengua casi muda,
testigos limpios de ánimo inocente,
que la curiosidad del elocuente.

Por aquesta razón de ti escuchado,
aunque me falten otras, ser meresco.   50
Lo que puedo te doy, y lo que he dado,
con recibillo tú yo me enriquesco.
De cuatro ninfas que del Tajo amado
salieron juntas, a cantar me ofresco,
Filódoce, Dinámene y Crimene,   55
Nise, que en hermosura par no tiene.

never let them think that fortune moves me
to abandon such a laudable intent;
Apollo and all of the nine muses
will give me time and make me eloquent   30
to tell the tiniest part of what you are,
using the very utmost of my power.

Meanwhile, I hope you won't mind if my theme is
the countryside and solitude you have loved,
and will not censure some imperfect parts   35
of my style, which I believe you once thought well of;
while serving in the bands of bloodthirsty Mars,
whose madness hardly ever is resisted,
I used what little time I could afford,
taking up now the pen and now the sword.   40

So to the rustic sound of my untutored
pipe please pay attention for a moment,
although it is unworthy of your ears,
bare as it is of grace and ornament,
for sometimes it can happen that one hears   45
a simple talent and a tongue unfluent
more gladly, as signs of a soul that's innocent,
than the rare inventions of the eloquent.

For that reason alone, if for no other,
I think I do deserve that you should hear me;   50
I give you what I can; if you receive it,
that is the greatest wealth that you can give me.
Four nymphs I propose as subject of my song,
who emerged together from beloved Tagus:
Phylodoce, Dynamene and Clymene   55
and Nise too, whose beauty has no equal.

Cerca del Tajo en soledad amena,
de verdes sauces hay una espesura,
toda de hiedra revestida y llena,
que por el tronco va hasta el altura,   60
y así la teje arriba y encadena,
que el sol no halla paso a la verdura;
el agua baña el prado, con sonido
alegrando la vista y el oído.

Con tanta mansedumbre el cristalino   65
Tajo en aquella parte caminaba,
que pudieran los ojos el camino
determinar apenas que llevaba.
Peinando sus cabellos de oro fino,
una ninfa, del agua, do moraba,   70
la cabeza sacó, y el prado ameno
vido de flores y de sombra lleno.

Movióla el sitio umbroso, el manso viento,
el suave olor de aquel florido suelo.
Las aves en el fresco apartamiento   75
vió descansar del trabajoso vuelo.
Secaba entonces el terreno aliento
el sol subido en la mitad del cielo.
En el silencio sólo se escuchaba
un susurro de abejas que sonaba.   80

Habiendo contemplado una gran pieza
atentamente aquel lugar sombrío,
somorgujó de nuevo su cabeza,
y al fondo se dejó calar del río.
A sus hermanas a contar empieza   85
del verde sitio el agradable frío,
y que vayan les ruega y amonesta
allí con su labor a estar la siesta.

Close by the Tagus, in pleasing solitude,
there is a stand of willows, a dense grove
all dressed and draped with ivy, whose multitude
of stems goes climbing to the top and weaves   60
a canopy thick enough to exclude
the sun, denying it access to green leaves
below; the sound of water fills this place,
making both plants and human ears rejoice.

In that part of its course the crystalline   65
Tagus moved so gently and so calmly
the eye was scarcely able to determine
in which direction it was smoothly flowing.
Combing hair that might have been made of fine
gold thread, a nymph from the stream that was her dwelling 70
stuck out her head and saw the delightful mead,
the flowers blooming and the abundant shade.

She was enchanted by the shady plot,
the gentle breeze, the subtle scents arising
from the flowery field; birds in that cool retreat   75
after the toil of flight she saw were resting;
the sun, which now had risen to its full height,
was soaking up the humors of the breathing
earth. In the silence the only thing she hears
is the slow whispered murmuring of bees.   80

Having quietly observed for a long while,
and considered every detail of the scene,
she dipped her head and slid again below,
letting herself sink swiftly to the bottom,
where she at once begins to tell them all   85
about the beauties of that spot, its green
shade; eagerly she exhorts each sister
to take her work and go there for the siesta.

No perdió en esto mucho tiempo el ruego,
que las tres dellas su labor tomaron,   90
y en mirando de fuera, vieron luego
el prado, hacia el cual enderezaron.
El agua clara con lacivo juego
nadando dividieron y cortaron,
hasta que el blanco pie tocó mojado,   95
saliendo de la arena, el verde prado.

Poniendo ya en lo enjuto las pisadas,
escurrieron del agua sus cabellos,
los cuales esparciendo, cubijadas
las hermosas espaldas fueron dellos.   100
Luego sacando telas delicadas,
que en delgadeza competían con ellos,
en lo más escondido se metieron,
y a su labor atentas se pusieron.

Las telas eran hechas y tejidas   105
del oro que el felice Tajo envía,
apurado, después de bien cernidas
las menudas arenas do se cría.
Y de las verdes hojas reducidas
en estambre sutil, cual convenía   110
para seguir el delicado estilo
del oro ya tirado en rico hilo.

La delicada estambre era distinta
de las colores que antes le habían dado
con la fineza de la varia tinta   115
que se halla en las conchas del pescado.
Tanto artificio muestra en lo que pinta
y teje cada ninfa en su labrado,
cuanto mostraron en sus tablas antes
el celebrado Apeles y Timantes.   120

There was no need for her to prolong her words,
for the three of them just took their work and rose   90
to the surface, where looking round they saw
the meadow and promptly headed for it;
sporting and leaping through the stream they went,
cleaving and splitting the transparent water,
until, after traversing the sandy shore,   95
still dripping wet, their white feet trod the greensward.

Now it is on dry land their footsteps fall,
as they shake the water from their streaming hair,
tossing and spreading it till it covers all
their lovely shoulders and their gleaming backs;   100
each nymph then taking out the delicate cloth
which rivals in its fineness her soft hair,
they settle themselves in the most hidden part
and devote themselves entirely to their art.

The fabric of the cloth that they were weaving   105
was made from gold the happy Tagus gives,
refined, after the sand which is its birthplace
is carefully panned or shaken out in sieves,
and also made from strands of green waterweed,
converted into a fine warp, which serves   110
to complement the delicate style that's bred
from gold spun out into a precious thread.

The threads they worked were delicate and fine,
subtly colored with many different tinctures,
using the various shades one can obtain   115
from their origin in shells of the sea's creatures.
Just as much art did each nymph demonstrate in
the composition of her woven pictures
as went in ancient times into the paintings
of the renowned Apelles and Timanthes.   120

Filódoce, que así de aquéllas era
llamada la mayor, con diestra mano
tenía figurada la ribera
de Estrimón, de una parte el verde llano,   125
y de otra el monte de aspereza fiera,
pisado tarde o nunca de pie humano,
donde el amor movió con tanta gracia
la dolorosa lengua del de Tracia.

Estaba figurada la hermosa
Eurídice, en el blanco pie mordida   130
de la pequeña sierpe ponzoñosa,
entre la hierba y flores escondida;
descolorida estaba como rosa
que ha sido fuera de sazón cogida,
y el ánima, los ojos ya volviendo,   135
de su hermosa carne despidiendo.

Figurado se vía estensamente
el osado marido que bajaba
al triste reino de la escura gente,
y la mujer perdida recobraba;   140
y cómo después desto él, impaciente
por miralla de nuevo, la tornaba
a perder otra vez, y del tirano
se queja al monte solitario en vano.

Dinámene no menos artificio   145
mostraba en la labor que había tejido,
pintando a Apolo en el robusto oficio
de la silvestre caza embebecido.
Mudar luego le hace el ejercicio
la vengativa mano de Cupido,   150
que hizo a Apolo consumirse en lloro
después que le enclavó con punta de oro.

Phylodoce, for of the eldest nymph
that was the name, had with a skillful hand
conjured up a view of the banks of Strymon,
on one side of which extended the green plain,
while on the other rose those rugged mountains,   125
seldom or never trodden by foot of human,
where love inspired with such bewitching grace
the hopeless song of the unhappy one from Thrace.

There pictured on the bank was the beautiful
Eurydice, whose fair white foot was bitten   130
by a poisonous snake that lurked, invisible,
among the grass, among the flowers hidden;
faded, she was, and pallid like a rose
that has been cultivated out of season;
and there above her, looking back, her soul   135
turning to bid the lovely flesh farewell.

The daring husband also could be seen,
and the whole story of his bold descent
into the gloomy realm of the shadowy ones,
from whence he brought the lost wife back again   140
and how he later, tempted by impatience
to look on her again, again must lose her,
and roam the lonely mountainside in vain
of underworld's cruel tyrant to complain.

In the design of the picture she had woven   145
Dynamene showed no less artifice:
She drew Apollo while engaged in the fine
and manly exercise of the woodland chase.
He is soon made to change this occupation
by Cupid's hand exercising vengeance   150
and consumes himself in tears, after being hit
by Cupid's arrow with the golden tip.

Dafne con el cabello suelto al viento,
sin perdonar al blanco pie, corría
por áspero camino tan sin tiento,   155
que Apolo en la pintura parecía
que, porque ella templase el movimiento,
con menos ligereza la seguía.
El va siguiendo, y ella huye como
quien siente al pecho el odioso plomo.   160

    Mas a la fin los brazos le crecían,
y en sendos ramos vueltos se mostraban,
y los cabellos, que vencer solían
al oro fino, en hojas se tornaban;
en torcidas raíces se estendían   165
los blancos pies, y en tierra se hincaban.
Llora el amante, y busca el ser primero,
besando y abrazando aquel madero.

    Climene, llena de destreza y maña,
el oro y las colores matizando,   170
iba de hayas una gran montaña
de robles y de peñas variando.
Un puerco entre ellas, de braveza estraña,
estaba los colmillos aguzando
contra un mozo, no menos animoso,   175
con su venablo en mano, que hermoso.

    Tras esto, el puerco allí se vía herido
de aquel mancebo por su mal valiente,
y el mozo en tierra estaba ya tendido,
abierto el pecho del rabioso diente;   180
con el cabello de oro desparcido
barriendo el suelo miserablemente,
las rosas blancas por allí sembradas
tornaba con su sangre coloradas.

Her hair streaming behind her, Daphne ran,
and showed no mercy to her own fair feet,
fleeing over rough ground with such abandon   155
that in the picture Apollo may be thought
to be pursuing less swiftly than he can,
in the hope she may become more circumspect;
while he pursues, she flees as one possessed,
with hatred's leaden arrow lodged in her breast.   160

But finally her arms began to grow
taking on the appearance of two boughs;
her hair meanwhile, which once used to outdo
pure gold for luster, was turning into leaves;
while her white feet extended into two   165
gnarled roots that thrust into the earth and gripped it;
the lover weeps and longs for her first form back,
as he hugs and kisses the unyielding bark.

Clymene, with style and virtuosity,
mixing the colored threads to shade the golden,   170
was adding interest to a mountain's outline
with trees, beeches and oaks, and scattered boulders;
there too a boar of rare ferocity
was sharpening the tusks he's going to wield
against a youth, as spirited and bold—   175
with spear in hand—as handsome to behold.

Next, you can see the boar has received its wound
from that young man, so careless of the risk,
and see him, too, lying shattered on the ground,
his breast torn open by the raging tusk   180
and wretchedly the golden locks around
his head despoiled and trailing in the dust;
the white roses that beautified that spot
were by his wasted blood all changed to scarlet.

Adonis éste se mostraba que era,   185
según se muestra Venus dolorida,
que viendo la herida abierta y fiera,
estaba sobre él casi amortecida.
Boca con boca coge la postrera
parte del aire que solía dar vida   190
al cuerpo, por quien ella en este suelo
aborrecido tuvo al alto cielo.

La blanca Nise no tomó a destajo
de los pasados casos la memoria,
y en la labor de su sutil trabajo   195
no quiso entretejer antigua historia;
antes mostrando de su claro Tajo
en su labor la celebrada gloria,
lo figuró en la parte donde él baña
la más felice tierra de la España.   200

Pintado el caudaloso río se vía,
que, en áspera estrecheza reducido,
un monte casi al rededor teñía,
con ímpetu corriendo y con ruído;
querer cercallo todo parecía   205
en su volver ; mas era afán perdido;
dejábase correr, en fin, derecho,
contento de lo mucho que había hecho.

Estaba puesta en la sublime cumbre
del monte, y desde allí por él sembrada,   210
aquella ilustre y clara pesadumbre,
de antiguos edificios adornada.
De allí con agradable mansedumbre
el Tajo va siguiendo su jornada,
y regando los campos y arboledas   215
con artificio de las altas ruedas.

That it was Adonis one could understand   185
by the way Venus was manifesting grief,
for when she saw the fearsome gaping wound
she fell on him almost bereft of sense.
Her mouth to his, she catches the very end
of all the air which previously blew life   190
into that flesh for which she'd gladly given
her own right of residence in heaven.

Fair Nise for her assignment did not take
the recording of cases from old history:
it was not antiquity she wished to make   195
the object of her subtle industry,
preferring in her work to show instead
her celebrated Tagus, in its glory,
depicting it where its waters entertain
the happiest region of the whole of Spain.   200

The mighty river in her picture's seen
reduced at this point to a rocky narrows,
surrounding almost on all sides a mountain,
and rushing along with energy and noise;
it seems to want, although the effort's vain,   205
to return upon itself again and close
the circle . . . but desists and runs straight on,
satisfied with the much that it has done.

Perched on the lofty brow of the great hill
and scattered down its slopes on every side,   210
was that incomparable and weighty pile,
with many an ancient edifice supplied.
From that point on, the Tagus is more tranquil
and will on its way more quietly proceed,
watering as it goes orchards and fields   215
with the ingenious aid of water-wheels.

En la hermosa tela se veían
entretejidas las silvestres diosas
salir de la espesura, y que venían
todas a la ribera presurosas,   220
en el semblante tristes, y traían
cestillos blancos de purpúreas rosas,
las cuales esparciendo, derramaban
sobre una ninfa muerta que lloraban.

Todas con el cabello desparcido   225
lloraban una ninfa delicada,
cuya vida mostraba que había sido
antes de tiempo y casi en flor cortada.
Cerca del agua, en un lugar florido,
estaba entre la hierba degollada,   230
cual queda el blanco cisne cuando pierde
la dulce vida entre la hierba verde.

Una de aquellas diosas, que en belleza,
al parecer, a todas ecedía,
mostrando en el semblante la tristeza   235
que del funesto y triste caso había,
apartada algún tanto, en la corteza
de un álamo unas letras escribía,
como epitafio de la ninfa bella,
que hablaban así por parte della: 240

"Elisa soy, en cuyo nombre suena
y se lamenta el monte cavernoso,
testigo del dolor y grave pena
en que por mí se aflige Nemoroso,
y llama Elisa; Elisa a boca llena   245
responde el Tajo, y lleva presuroso
al mar de Lusitania el nombre mío,
donde será escuchado, yo lo fío."

On this beautiful canvas she had woven,
the sylvan deities, the spirits of nature,
were seen emerging from the undergrowth
and hurrying down toward the riverside,   220
their countenances somber; in their hands
they bore white baskets filled to the brim with crimson
roses, which they were scattering and pouring
over a dead nymph whom they were mourning.

Their hair disshevelled, trailing in disarray,   225
they are all mourning a tender nymph, whose life
has clearly been cut short before its day,
just as the bud was coming into flower;
In a dappled place beside the stream she lay,
bloodless, limp, lodged in a leafy bower;   230
like the white swan, when sweet life is ended,
cast on the green grass like a thing discarded.

One of those fair goddesses, whose beauty
seemed to exceed that of all the rest,
her countenance expressing the great pity   235
aroused by such a sorrowful event,
standing a little to one side, was busy
carving on the bark of a tree a text,
which was to be the fair nymph's epitaph,
delivering these words on her behalf: 240

"Elisa am I, and to my unlucky name
the cave-infested mountain echoes and moans,
witness to the grief, the overwhelming pain
Nemoroso must suffer on my account:
'Elisa,' he calls out, and 'Elisa' again   245
Tagus intones, as it rushes swiftly on,
bearing my name to the Lusitanian sea,
to where it will be heard, I can safely say."

En fin, en esta tela artificiosa
toda la historia estaba figurada,   250
que en aquella ribera deleitosa
de Nemoroso fué tan celebrada;
porque de todo aquesto y cada cosa
estaba Nise ya tan informada,
que llorando el pastor, mil veces ella   255
se enterneció escuchando su querella.

Y porque aqueste lamentable cuento,
no sólo entre las selvas se contase,
mas, dentro de las ondas, sentimiento
con la noticia de esto se mostrase,   260
quiso que de su tela el argumento
la bella ninfa muerta señalase,
y así se publicase de uno en uno
por el húmido reino de Netuno.

Destas historias tales variadas   265
eran las telas de las cuatro hermanas,
las cuales, con colores matizadas
y claras luces de las sombras vanas,
mostraban a los ojos relevadas
las cosas y figuras que eran llanas;   270
tanto que, al parecer, el cuerpo vano
pudiera ser tomado con la mano.

Los rayos ya del sol se trastornaban,
escondiendo su luz, al mundo cara,
tras altos montes, y á la luna daban   275
lugar para mostrar su blanca cara;
los peces a menudo ya saltaban,
con la cola azotando el agua clara,
cuando las ninfas, la labor dejando,
hacia el agua se fueron paseando.   280

This ingenious tapestry, in a word,
illustrated the whole story that had been   250
the talk of all the pleasant riverside,
concerning Nemoroso's sad misfortune;
for the way of it and of much else beside
to Nise is already so well known
that when the shepherd mourns, each time she hears   255
his lamentation, she too is moved to tears.

In order to warrant that the dreadful tale
not only should be told among the forests,
but that its telling should gain sympathy
equally in the world beneath the waves,   260
she had planned that the subject of her tapestry
would single out the beautiful dead nymph,
so that from mouth to mouth the news relayed
should fill the humid realm where Neptune reigned.

Such are the varied stories that were told   265
in the fine tapestries of these four sisters,
who joined their colors in an artful blend,
with highlights that from the empty shadows
brought forward, as if standing in the round,
objects and figures that were flat and so   270
you'd think that empty forms were solid and
could actually be taken in the hand.

Now the rays of the sun would soon be gone,
hiding the light that to our world's so precious
behind high mountains, and offering the moon   275
a chance to show her beautiful white face;
the fish were rising now in quick succession,
whipping the limpid water with their tails,
as the four sisters put away their work
and set off walking down to the river bank.   280

En las templadas ondas ya metidos
tenían los pies, y reclinar querían
los blancos cuerpos, cuando sus oídos
fueron de dos zampoñas que tañían
suave y dulcemente, detenidos;   285
tanto, que sin mudarse las oían,
y al son de las zampoñas escuchaban
dos pastores, a veces, que cantaban.

Más claro cada vez el son se oía
de dos pastores, que venían cantando   290
tras el ganado, que también venía
por aquel verde soto caminando,
y a la majada, ya pasado el día,
recogido llevaban, alegrando
las verdes selvas con el son suave,   295
haciendo su trabajo menos grave.

Tirreno destos dos el uno era,
Alcino el otro, entrambos estimados,
y sobre cuantos pacen la ribera
del Tajo, con sus vacas, enseñados;   300
mancebos de una edad, de una manera
a cantar juntamente aparejados,
y a responder. Aquesto van diciendo,
cantando el uno, el otro respondiendo.

Tirreno
        Flérida, para mí dulce y sabrosa   305
más que la fruta del cercado ajeno,
más blanca que la leche y más hermosa
que el prado por Abril, de flores lleno;
si tú respondes pura y amorosa
al verdadero amor de tu Tirreno,   310

Their feet had already entered the warm flood,
and they were about to stretch out and give back
their white bodies to the water, when they heard
the dulcet sound of two country flutes, which struck
the ear so arrestingly that where they stood   285
by this sweet music they were held in check:
two shepherds' voices also they were hearing,
one song in alternating verses sharing.

Ever more clearly now the song was heard
of two shepherds, singing as they went along   290
behind their animals, which likewise strayed
through the green spinneys, and heading now for home
with their flock, which since the day was done
they'd rounded up and were driving to the fold,
gladdening the greenwood with their sweet song,   295
making their work as well less burdensome.

One of the two Tirreno was by name,
Alcino the other, both much esteemed
and among all those who on the banks of Tagus
grazed their sheep the brightest and best informed,   300
both of an age and both for taking part in
this kind of singing equally well endowed.
This is what they sang, one first proposing,
the other, next, to what he sang responding.

Tirreno
Flerida, for me, sweeter, more alluring   305
than forbidden fruit in a neighbor's orchard,
whiter than fresh milk and more entrancing
than April meadows filled with new spring flowers;
if you respond with a heart that's pure and loving
to Tirreno's love, which is all truly yours,   310

a mi majada arribarás, primero
que el cielo nos amuestre su lucero.

Alcino
    Hermosa Filis, siempre yo te sea
amargo al gusto más que la retama,
y de ti despojado yo me vea,   315
cual queda el tronco de su verde rama,
si más que yo el murciélago desea
la escuridad, ni más la luz desama,
por ver ya el fin de un término tamaño
deste día, para mí mayor que un año.   320

Tirreno
    Cual suele acompañada de su bando
aparecer la dulce primavera,
cuando Favonio y Céfiro soplando,
al campo tornan su beldad primera,
y van artificiosos esmaltando   325
de rojo, azul y blanco la ribera;
en tal manera a mí, Flérida mía,
viniendo, reverdece mi alegría.

Alcino
    ¿Ves el furor del animoso viento,
embravecido en la fragosa sierra,   330
que los antiguos robles ciento a ciento
y los pinos altísimos atierra,
y de tanto destrozo aún no contento,
al espantoso mar mueve la guerra?
Pequeña es esta furia, comparada   335
a la de Filis, con Alcino airada.

at the sheepfold I know you will appear
before in the sky we see the evening star.

Alcino
Fair Phyllis, it is my wish that I may be
more bitter to your taste than prickly furze,
and all your love be taken away from me   315
like a tree when it is stripped of its green boughs,
if it be true the bat more longs to see
night come, or is to daylight more averse
than I, who await the end of such a day
as this, which seems interminably to stay.   320

Tirreno
Just as when spring with all her retinue
sweetly appears, to gladden the world once more,
when Favonius and Zephyr softly blow
and to the fields their former grace restore,
and clothe the banks in red and white and blue,   325
with artful colors enamelling the floor,
just so it is that when my Flerida comes
my happiness revives again and blooms.

Alcino
Do you see the fury of the blustering wind
that rages on the rugged mountain tops,   330
and tallest pines brings crashing to the ground
and in their hundreds fells the ancient oaks,
and with this havoc still not satisfied
on the fearsome ocean launches its attack?
All this is nothing if compared to Phyllis,   335
when she with her Alcino is displeased.

Tirreno
El blanco trigo multiplica y crece,
produce el campo en abundancia tierno
pasto al ganado, el verde monte ofrece
a las fieras salvajes su gobierno;   340
adoquiera que miro me parece
que derrama la copia todo el cuerno;
mas todo se convertirá en abrojos
si dello aparta Flérida sus ojos.

Alcino
De la esterilidad es oprimido   345
el monte, el campo, el soto y el ganado;
la malicia del aire corrompido
hace morir la hierba mal su grado;
las aves ven su descubierto nido,
que ya de verdes hojas fué cercado;   350
pero si Filis por aquí tornare,
hará reverdecer cuanto mirare.

Tirreno
El álamo de Alcides escogido
fué siempre, y el laurel del rojo Apolo;
de la hermosa Venus fué tenido   355
en precio y en estima el mirto solo;
el verde sauz de Flérida es querido,
y por suyo entre todos escogiólo;
doquiera que de hoy más sauces se hallen,
el álamo, el laurel y el mirto callen.   360

Alcino
El fresno por la selva en hermosura
sabemos ya que sobre todos vaya,
y en aspereza y monte de espesura
se aventaja la verde y alta haya;

Tirreno

The pale wheat multiplies and grows and grows,
the fields produce in generous abundance
feed for the livestock, while the green hills offer
to wild beasts all they need for sustenance;   340
it seems, whichever way I turn my eyes,
that plenty's horn is spilling all its contents,
yet all will turn into a desert waste,
if Flerida withdraws her lovely gaze.

Alcino

With barrenness the mountain is afflicted,   345
likewise all the fields, woods and livestock;
some malignancy by which the air's infected,
willy-nilly is killing off the grass;
the birds find their nests have been detected
despite green leaves by which they were encompassed;   350
but it only needs that Phyllis should return,
with just one look to make everything turn green.

Tirreno

The poplar was the choice of Hercules,
always; the laurel was red Apollo's tree;
by beautiful Venus no tree but the myrtle   355
was held to be of value and esteemed;
what Flerida loves is the green, green willow,
which she chose above all others as her tree;
from today, wherever willows most abound,
let poplar, laurel, myrtle yield their ground.   360

Alcino

In the forest the beauty of the ash tree
is superior to all others, as we know,
and in the harsh and tangled wilderness
the tall and leafy beech makes a great show;

mas el que la beldad de tu figura   365
dondequiera mirado, Filis, haya,
al fresno y a la haya en su aspereza
confesará que vence tu belleza.—

 Esto cantó Tirreno, y esto Alcino
le respondió; y habiendo ya acabado   370
el dulce son, siguieron su camino
con paso un poco más apresurado.
Siendo a las ninfas ya el rumor vecino,
todas juntas se arrojan por el vado,
y de la blanca espuma que movieron   375
las cristalinas hondas se cubrieron.

but he, Phyllis, who's once had the good fortune   365
to see your face, gives the victory to you,
and in a contest where nature has no chance,
deems the rough beech and ash not worth a glance.

Thus Tirreno sang and thus responded
Alcino, and when the sweet sound sank to silence   370
the singers once again proceeded onward
with a certain quickening of their pace;
sensing them close at hand, the nymphs, alarmed,
dived and swam away beneath the surface;
on the crystal water nothing now was seen   375
but a circle of white foam where they had been.

Appendix A

TWO COPLAS
The first of these two coplas by Garcilaso is the one to which were added in one manuscript the words: "To doña Isabel Freyre, because she married a man who was beneath her." I have no idea, especially in the case of Copla IV, whether my attempted translation comes anywhere near the meaning, which I find quite obscure: I hope though it is sufficient to give an idea of what is going on. The short, choppy lines and repetitive language are very different from the flowing Italianate verse.

I have not attempted the rhyming, which is *abbab cdcdcabbab.*

COPLA II

When his lady married

To love you must be a fault,
since you treat me as you do,
but later you'll pay the price—
when you are disregarded—
for your disregard of me.

I thought to die for loving,
but not to suffer blame;
both fates it seems are mine,
as you have shown to me

and but too well I know.
Would that I did not love you,
as you know too well I do,
and could enjoy the knowing
that disregards the pay-off
for your disregard of me.

COPLA IV

On a parting

It was, in my view, by chance
he rightly chose to love you
when he made such a bad choice
deciding he would leave you
and lose the sight of you.

Impossible such as he,
if he had truly known you,
should know what he was doing,
when his happiness and pain
he surrendered the same day.
It was by chance he did it,
this thing, that had he known you
he never could achieve:
to leave you once he'd seen you,
and never see you more.

Appendix B

Garcilaso's letter, which was used as a prologue to Boscán's translation of *The Courtier* by Castiglione (whose name was rendered in Spanish as Castellón).

To the most great lady doña Gerónima Palova de Almogávar
Had I not known beforehand the extent of your grace's judgement, the fact that you like this book would have been enough to persuade me of it. But you already stood so high in my opinion that the chief of many reasons for which I like the book seems to me now your having liked it so much that we can say you made it, since it is through you that we have acquired it in the language we understand. For not only did I think I could never persuade Boscán to translate it, but I did not even dare suggest it to him, so strongly had I seen him object to those who vulgarize books by turning them into the vernacular; though neither he nor I would call this vulgarizing and even if it were, I believe he would not be able to refuse when the request came from you.

I am well pleased with myself for having esteemed the book as I ought before it came into your hands, for if I should start to recognize it now, after it has received your approval, it might be thought that I was influenced by your opinion. But now there can be no question of this, but only the certainty that it is a book which deserves to be in your hands so that it can advertise where it has been and hereafter travel the world with confidence. Because one of the most important things, wherever there are ladies and gentlemen of the first rank, is not only to do everything that in their way of life increases their personal value and worth, but even more to avoid everything that can lower it; both are dealt with in this book so wisely and gracefully that I think there is nothing to wish for but to see it all realized in some man, and I was also going to say some lady, if I had not remembered that you are here to call me to account for unnecessary words. Besides all this, it can be said of this book that just as the best ideas always exceed what they promise, Count Castellón wrote so well about how an excellent courtier should behave that he scarcely left any condition of men without advice about their office. From this we can see how much we should lose by not having it.

I also consider as major the benefit bestowed on the Castillian language by translating into it things that deserve to be read, because, although I know not why we have always been so unlucky, scarcely anything has been written in our language but things we could do without (though it would be hard to convince those who are addicted to those dangerous books that speak of killing). And you were very successful in your choice of the person who was to bring us all this benefit, because I think it as difficult to translate a book well as to write it, and Boscán was so skilful in this that every time I read this book of his, or rather yours, it does not seem as if written in another language; and if for a moment my mind goes back to the original, which I have read, it returns immediately to the one I have in my hands. He achieved something in Castillian that very few have managed, which was to avoid affectation, without falling into dryness, and together with great purity of style he used very courtly terms, such as are admitted by those of good taste and are neither new nor unfamiliar to ordinary people. He was, moreover, a very faithful translator, because he did not follow the literal sense, as some do, but the true meaning, and used different ways to convey in this language all the force and ornament of the other, leaving it all in as good order as he found it, having interpreted it so well that it is very easy for the defenders of the book to reply to those who would wish to delete something from it.

I do not speak of those who have such tender and delicate ears that among a thousand good things there may be in this book, they will be offended by one or two that are inferior to the rest, because people such as these, I cannot help thinking, really enjoy those one or two things and it is the rest they do not like; and I could prove this from many of the things they like apart from this. But there is no point in wasting time with them, better to leave them to those who can talk to them and answer them on their own terms. I shall return to those who with some semblance of reason can in one matter complain of something which offends them, which is that where it deals with all the ways of telling jokes and devising witticisms for the sake of laughter and fine talk, there are some examples which do not reach the same standard as the rest nor do they deserve to be esteemed by one who dealt so intelligently with the other parts; and from this they might suspect the author of not having such good judgement or such delicacy as we ascribed to him. To this it could be replied that the intention of the author was to show different ways of speaking humorously and telling jokes, and in order that we could recognize the difference and the nature of each of these ways he gave us examples of them all. And since he dealt with so many ways of speaking there could not be so many well-said things in each that some of the examples he gave were not lower than others; and I believe he saw them as such, without for a moment being deceived in it, being such an intelligent and discriminating writer. So in this too we can see he is not to blame. I will have to admit to just one fault myself, which is having gone on longer than necessary, but I do not like injustices and they have made me incur a fault with such a long letter to one who is not to blame.

I confess to your grace that I was so envious of seeing you deserve all the thanks due for this book that I wanted to get into the act by inserting myself between the lines, or whatever way I could. And because I feared that someone else might seek to translate it or (better say) spoil it, I urged Boscán to have it printed without delay, to forestall the haste which those who write badly have to publish. And although this publication would avenge any other there might be, I am so opposed to discord that even such a minor one as this would upset me, and so I almost forced him to get it done with all speed and he involved me in the final polishing, more as someone receptive to reason than for my assistance in any corrections. I beg you, since this book is under your protection, that it should lose nothing by this small part that I take in it, since in return I give it to you more clearly written, that your name and good works may be appreciated.

Notes

INTRODUCTION TO THE SONNETS

For the dating and stylistic development of Garcilaso's poetry, the classical study is Rafael Lapesa's *La trayectoria poética de Garcilaso*.

SONNET I

Line 2: Rivers has the verb in the plural ("han Traído") to agree with "pasos," which seems to make better sense.

Line 7: From this point on, the repetition of *acabar* with slightly varying meanings, and use of *saber/querer/poder* with a similar meaning is a mark of the old, *cancionero* style.

Lines 7–8: "Care" would be the direct translation of *cuidado*, a conventional way of referring to love and its attendant suffering in poetry of the period. In modern English, however, I think "care" sounds negative, in other words not something you might regret the loss of. Superficially there is some similarity to Sonnet XXIX on Leander (not included here), who, drowning, is "more pained by (thinking of) the happiness he would lose by dying than by (losing) his own life" ("más del bien que allí perdía muriendo / que de su propia vida congojoso"). But there is no suggestion here of the love ever being returned—quite the opposite.

Line 9: He handed himself over naively, *sin arte*: the poetic conceit of the true (male) lover's helplessness in the face of duplicity.

Lines 9–14: The sestet is particularly reminiscent of the older poetry, but the use of such elements of style as a touchstone for Garcilaso's poetic development should not detract from the neatness of the idea: he is finished because he has handed himself over to one who can kill him if she wants, and probably she will want to. Why? Because even he can decide to kill himself, and she is less "on his side" than he is. One of various implications is that he may have willed his own death by falling in love with her (a fatal attraction, in fact).

Line 14: This is about as close to word-for-word translation as one could get and sounds awkward in both languages.

Sonnet V

I made many versions of this sonnet, none entirely satisfactory. The imagery is not unusual or original, but there seems to be more going on than at first meets the eye, despite its being made up mainly of straightforward statements that individually could be taken as a direct expression of romantic love. Reading it as an example of neoplatonism one may be reminded that in the Christian catechism man is born to love and to serve God and see the poem as equating love and religion. I tried to preserve both the emphatic tone and the ambivalence.

Line 4: "Fearful," because he regards her with an almost religious respect.

Lines 5–8: These lines are not entirely clear but seem to introduce the familiar opposition between faith and reason.

Lines 9–12: Quoted out of context, line 9 might do well as a modern valentine; but the following image sounds almost aggressive. The "habit" in line 12 is both something to wear and behavior that cannot be eradicated. The image occurs also in Sonnet XXVII:

> O Love, o Love, I made myself a habit,
> a costume cut entirely from your cloth;
> when first I put it on it seemed to fit,
> but, wearing it a while, I found it tight.

This follows almost literally the closing lines of a poem by Ausías March (Canto LII in Montemayor's Spanish translation).

Sonnet X

The contrast between past happiness and present misery is a recurring theme in Garcilaso's poetry.

Lines 1–2: *Prendas*, which I translate as "mementoes," is quite vague. It could mean anything that belonged to the loved one, such as a lock of hair or piece of clothing. It is often thought to refer here to a souvenir of Isabel Freyre, but the two opening lines also quote Dido's speech (*Aeneid IV*, 807–9) on seeing Aeneas' clothes and the bed they slept in, just before she kills herself. Garcilaso simply changes "Fate and the gods" to "God."

Line 6: *Bien,* "good" (as noun), here and in line 10, is another very general word, which Garcilaso uses in various ways. Here it is balanced by *dolor,* "pain," in line 8 and *mal,* "ill, evil," in line 11, so the simplest translation for the two is happiness and pain. I think it is partly because such simple terms are unspecific and imprecise that we often have with Garcilaso the sense of some wider meaning than the immediate context requires.

Line 8: In the Spanish, the meaning of *representadas* is given by its two parts—re-presented, offered to me again.

SONNET XI

Line 1: In the original the nymphs are simply beautiful (*hermosas*) but I discarded that overworked word because I wanted to capture the glamour that I think surrounds them. The trappings of classicism must have been fresher to Garcilaso and his contemporaries than they are to us.

Line 11: The phrase *según ando,* "according to how I am," is thoroughly inexplicit, though it obviously implies unhappiness.

Line 12: It is not entirely clear to me why pity should make them *not* able to listen to him, rather than the reverse, but he definitely says this is one of the reasons why he will not take up much of their time. I suppose it is just hyperbole: his tale is *unbearably* sad.

Lines 13–14: This is not the only place where Garcilaso equates death with melting or drowning (see, for example, Song III). On the other hand, we only assume he means death because of the implication that he will be joining the nymphs *allá,* "there," under the water (*allá* also has connotations of "in the next world"). The mixture of hyperbole and reticence, or understatement, is very typical of Garcilaso.

SONNET XIII

This sonnet on Daphne draws on Ovid's *Metamorphoses.* Garcilaso returns to this subject in Eclogue III, stanzas 20–21. The greater number of adjectives marks it as belonging to his later style. They are conventional—green leaves, white feet, and so on— as tends to be the case in Spanish when the adjective is placed before the noun, not after it, and they contribute more to the flow of the verse than the meaning.

Line 3 (line 4 in the Spanish): In the Spanish her hair "darkened gold" ("el oro escurecían"), a conventional way of describing beautiful hair.

Line 4 (line 3 in the Spanish): By including himself as observer the poet seems, as a novelist might, to insist on the authenticity of what he describes.

Lines 12–14: We may wonder if the idea that we can be a major cause of our own suffering had personal significance for Garcilaso. He repeats this idea elsewhere, and it might have relevance to the self-condemnation in Song III, line 19.

SONNET XVII

Lines 12–14: This seems to be a variation on Garcilaso's usual theme that the past was better than the present: in this case the past was simply less painful.

SONNET XXIII

Line 1: The hanging clauses in the two quatrains are completed by the imperative at the start of line 9. Poems on the carpe diem theme (as this is) are cast as advice (generally the reverse of disinterested).

Line 4: Some editions have Garcilaso's earlier version of this line: "enciende el corazón y lo refrena" ("stirs up passion and holds it back" or, as I originally translated it to save the rhyme, "passion's fires both foster and oppose"), which exactly parallels the slightly paradoxical "ardiente y honesta" ("ardent and chaste").

Line 11: Snow and mountain peaks are conventional images for the white hair of old age.

SONNET XXV

Line 5: The narrow space is a grave, as line 9 makes explicit. I have cheated a little by adding "unbounded," but I needed the extra syllables and a broader rhythm, and I felt the contrast was implicit in the plural "amores" and the lifting rhythm of the following line. Those who favor biographical explanations will assume it is the grave of Isabel Freyre, which Garcilaso could have visited on one of the occasions when he returned to Spain on military or diplomatic missions. There are however some questions: the ashes it contains are "disdainful, cold/ and deaf to my complaints and to my cries," which is reminiscent of the language of the eclogues, but not quite appropriate to the feelings of a romantic lover mourning one who has died. And they are ashes not just of his "amores" but also of "toda la esperanza de mis cosas," "all the hope of my affairs." Does this suggest that the roots of his pain are set as much in frustrated ambition as unhappy love? My translation of this as "all the hopes I ever had" favors this meaning, but I have to admit the language is too vague to fully support it.

Line 11: Once again the simple word "allá," "there," appears with gloomy connotations. But whoever it may be in that grave, the speaker is now addressing them.

Line 12: The phrase "aquella eterna noche escura" is far removed from the conventional Christian gloss on death as a release from suffering and entry into heaven.

Line 14: The subjunctive gives a purposive twist to the last line that is difficult to guarantee in English. "Shall see" sounds too triumphant and "will see" too definite about the future.

SONNET XXX

Line 1: The suspicions are about the faithfulness of a lover; the subject is jealousy, as in Elegy II.

Lines 3–4: In the Spanish the pain is located in the breast. I have changed this to "head" partly for the half rhyme and partly to bring it more into line with modern English usage: the head seems a more plausible location for suspicion, even when what it really means is jealousy.

Lines 9–10: More literally "that so fearful place." It can be compared with the "place full of shame and grief" of Elegy II, line 111. Ostensibly both passages refer to the pain of jealousy and the "death" that comes about when jealous fears are verified. But the emotion seems to overflow the conventional frame.

SONNET XXXII

Line 3: More literally "I dare not tell you," which suggests more clearly the courtly prohibition on telling one's love (but misses the rhyme).

Lines 5–10: I do not suppose any connection, but these lines bring to mind the dangerous journeys that Spaniards were making over deserts and mountains in the New World.

Lines 12–14: The magnificent ending gives what could seem a tired poetic convention a universal resonance.

SONNET XXXIII

The caption is probably an editorial addition. Garcilaso makes light of his battle wounds, wittily turning a real event into an incident in love's wars. There is a conventional basis for this in a multitude of Renaissance poems that treat Love, or Cupid, as a feared enemy (or pretend to do so). But more importantly, I think, we may be reminded of the advice in Castiglione's book (p. 67) that the courtier should make difficult accomplishments appear easy and practice nonchalance (Castiglione's term is *sprezzatura*).

Line 7 (Spanish): In Navarro Tomás it is "mi crueza," but that does not seem to make sense.

SONNET XXXV

Heading: La Goleta was near Tunis and close to the site of ancient Carthage in North Africa. Charles V had just won his victory over Barbarossa there.

Line 2: I have added "modern" to emphasize the parallel with the Roman power, subject of the second quatrain.

Line 5: "Reducir" is used here as elsewhere in golden age poetry in its original Latin sense of "bring back." "Reverdear," in the preceding line, and perhaps "revuelve" in line 12 draw attention to repeating cycles. The sonnet progresses backward in time: from the present, with Charles V's destruction of Tunis; to the Roman past and the wars which destroyed Carthage, in lines 5–11; and in the last two lines further back still to mythology and the death of Dido consequent on her abandonment by Aeneas, the founder of Rome.

Line 12: The same phrase, "vuelve y revuelve," is used (in participle form) in Sonnet XXX. I have translated it differently in the two poems because I feel the reduplicating sound is more important than the precise sense. Although the phrase suggests mental pain in both cases, here it also continues the notion of history repeating itself.

Line 13: "Hiere y enciende," "wounds and sets fire to," echoes the description of Dido's plight at the beginning of book 4 of the Aeneid and the "tears and ashes" of the following line may remind us of her end on the funeral pyre. For more on this sonnet (six brief but very suggestive chapters) see Helgerson.

SONNET XXXVII

This separation of tongue and self is curious and a little like the separation of self and body that Albanio experiences in the second eclogue.

Lines 1–2: The repetitive syllables in "do el dolor" and "ya yo" have been criticized as ugly, but the latter has also been praised by a different commentator as onomatopoeic for a cry of pain and I suppose one might hear the former as a kind of stutter.

Lines 7–8: His tongue is "she" because the noun is feminine in Spanish, and saying "more than she ought" refers presumably to the troubador prohibition on speaking your love.

SONG III

Line 6 (English 5–6): A reference to his being imprisoned on the island.

Lines 17–19: A note in Elias Rivers suggests these lines are proof that Garcilaso recognizes his guilt in the affair of the secret marriage. It seems to me just as likely to represent the persona of the desperate lover, or even perhaps to express a stoic acceptance of injustice.

Line 19: More literally, "someone who condemns himself."

Lines 25–26: This says, more literally, "I die only for that which I hope (or expect) to die for." It probably refers to the tradition in love poetry that love is fatal and leads to the death of the lover. But as so often in Garcilaso's poetry it seems also to have wider implications.

Lines 27–32: This is generally taken to refer to the emperor, Charles V. As his subject, Garcilaso would be in his power anyway, but he was also directly in his service. His present situation is further proof of his powerlessness. I find the tone of stanzas 3 and 4 hard to judge. Is it angry, bitter, defiant, or resigned? The general meaning, however, is "I am dying of love and nothing else really matters to me."

Line 29: More literally, "do as he likes whatever he pleases," but I introduced "heart" for the rhyme.

Line 32: "My other part" ("otra prenda") seems to refer to the soul, but it is notable that he does not use the word for soul, "alma," and the whole passage is indirect. As in Sonnet I, Garcilaso uses simple terms that give no clear definition of the causes of his unhappiness: the word for death or dying is used six times directly, and "mal" (unhappiness, evil, death) occurs more than once.

Line 34: This ("the final throw of the dice") is a slight mistranslation as it really means death, the "final fate," but I think the translation does not betray the mood.

Line 38: The original is more oblique, literally, "finds me and has found me." Garcilaso is fond of these elaborations of tense (for example, in sonnet XXV he has "are spilt today and were spilt"). The significance of repeating the verb in present and past tense is not always clear.

Line 39: This dry, understated reference to the pain of love is typical of Garcilaso.

Lines 44–45: Garcilaso does not tell us what exactly it is that has been destroyed ("todo aquello . . ./ en que toda mi vida fue gastada," "all that / on which all my life was spent."

Line 46: "Jornada" from its literal sense of what can be done in a day acquires the sense of a journey and also of fighting or a battle or campaign.

Lines 48–49: In the Spanish, the repetitive syllables draw attention to the oddity of this double negative: "no puedo / morir sino sin miedo," "I cannot die except without fear."

Line 54: The "fieras naciones" could be proud nations as well as fierce nations. However, "fierce" might suggest wrongly that he fears them; I preferred "savage" because I think rather that they are both alien and somewhat exotic to him.

Line 65: I believe the word "error" here combines the senses of mistake and wandering. It is Petrarchan to speak of love as error.

Lines 66–71: All but the last of Garcilaso's five songs end with an address to the personified song, as do many of Petrarch's. The reference to songs that did not pass his lips (literally, that died in his mouth) is probably a leftover from the courtly love tradition, in which a lover is not supposed to divulge his love.

Line 73: More literally, "you will hear it from me there" ("allá"). This is vague, but very close to the modern Spanish en el más allá, "in the afterlife." I was going to translate it as "when we meet in the

beyond," but that makes the reference to death a little too direct.
"Beyond the stream" seemed closer to Garcilaso's imagination, much
preoccupied with death and water (compare also Sonnet XI).

SONG V

Lines 1–10: The story of Orpheus with his lyre, which could con-
trol nature, is a familiar Renaissance analogy for poetry and its power.
Line 5: In the original the stronger word, "fury," precedes the
weaker, "movement," which might seem to be the wrong way round.
But in the context of calming things down, it is quite logical. In
repeating the word "sea" I tried to find an equivalent for an effect that
seems typical of this poem: in many stanzas the longer final line ends
with a phrase that sounds like something tacked on repetitively, which
for me gives the whole poem something of the sound of waves.

Lines 13–15: Garcilaso uses "convertido" in a Latin sense of
"turned towards" (not "converted"). Mars, god of war, "stained with
powder, blood and sweat," is much more than a dead classical figure
to Garcilaso. He may also be using "teñido" with an original Latin
sense of "moistened" or "soaked," but "stained" seems to me to fit the
context.

Lines 16–20: Literally the captains are "placed on sublime wheels,"
but they could also be "in high circles or spheres." The Spanish "rue-
das" allows either meaning and both are relevant. The captains are
taken from classical imagery, riding in chariots for a victory parade or
Roman triumph, and are thus symbolic. But there is also a contempo-
rary reference: Charles V had recently defeated the Protestant league in
Germany and earlier captured the king of France and sacked Rome. He
had been crowned emperor in Bologna in 1530, after a triumphal entry
into the city, and saw himself as the inheritor of Roman imperial glory.

Lines 28–30: The lover is turned into a violet, probably because
he is pale and weak, but Violet, or Violante, is also the woman's name.
Possibly "en tu figura" ("in your face or figure") means he has taken
on her likeness, the likeness of a violet. I have given what seems the
simplest interpretation.

Lines 31–35: Mario Galeota is the captive. This must have been a
more recognizable and compelling image at a time when galleys rowed
by slaves were so important to the competing powers in the Mediter-
ranean, whether Christian or Muslim, states or pirates.

Lines 36–45: Horsemanship and tilting in the lists were considered important aspects of training for battle. In a later generation Góngora satirizes courtiers for abandoning the lists owing to idleness, rather than the demands of a lover.

Lines 51–60: The friend is Garcilaso. An unrequited lover is a difficult friend, a psychological detail that goes a little beyond conventional accounts of unhappy love. There is surely some humor in Garcilaso's not disinterested plea for the woman to treat his friend better.

Lines 61–62: The "hard earth" is said to be a reference to the myth of Cadmus and the warriors, who were made out of earth.

Lines 66–100: Anaxarete is from Ovid's *Metamorphoses*. Her story, like Daphne's (Sonnet X and Eclogue III) shows a person becoming a thing.

Line 70: Apart from adding "flesh" I have translated this literally. It is hard to see how marble can burn, but I am sure the allusion is not to a tombstone (as it might be elsewhere) but to her beauty and coldness.

Line 80: The punishment he procures is hers, not his, though from a Christian point of view his suicide would be condemned—further evidence of the extent to which Garcilaso takes on classical ideas in preference to Christian. It is in fact a reversal of the language of Christianity: Christ with his death purchased man's redemption, while here the young man purchases Anaxarete's damnation.

ELEGY I

Line 14: The Muses.

Lines 22–24: This tercet includes two problematic words: "entrails," which will not fit easily into a romantic or even a heroic context, and "tears," which modern ears soon weary of. I have dealt with them as best I can. In fact, for Garcilaso the idea of melting in tears seems something more than a conventional reference to grief (see Sonnet XI and Song III).

Lines 25–36: This seems to me a vivid and psychologically accurate observation. I suspect Garcilaso may have been influenced by something in his reading, but the search for psychological realism is a constant in his poetry.

Line 38 (Spanish 39): Trápana or Trapani is the place in Sicily where the emperor's army rested after the Tunisian campaign (see Sonnet XXXV and Elegy II).

Lines 46–50: Lampetia mourned her brother Phaethon, who died when he drove Apollo's chariot too near the sun. The Eridanus, one of the rivers of the underworld, is said to be the river Po in northern Italy.

Line 56: "She lay her down": this breaks my rule about not using archaic forms but I allowed it because of Garcilaso's more elevated language here and the artificial nature of the piece.

Lines 58–61: Garcilaso himself had lost a younger brother, who died of illness during the siege of Naples by the French in 1528.

Line 69: There is more than one possible meaning for this, but to me it suggests a compliment to both brothers: the elder brother's opinions fell on fertile ground because don Bernaldino's nature also was noble.

Lines 82–92: This outburst against war must surely be rooted in Garcilaso's own experience.

Line 96: I have supplied the capital letter, in accordance with English usage, since I can see no other suitable referent but God.

Lines 97–98: The "enemy of the human race" is Death (not Satan).

Line 101: This line reveals that don Bernaldino is being addressed.

Line 129: I have added "calm felicity," which I think is implied by the calm beauty of this passage. There is a deliberate contrast between this image and the description of the mother's and sisters' violent grief that follows it.

Line 142: The Tormes is the river that runs through Salamanca, but before that on its way down from the mountains it passes through Alba de Tormes, home of the dukes of Alba. Classical iconography represents a river as a bearded man leaning on an urn from which water is pouring.

Lines 175–77: These lines cannot logically address the nymphs (who are being chased), although they were addressed along with satyrs and fauns in line 169. The sensuality of this passage may seem faintly surprising in the elegiac context. A similar note is sounded in the passage on Venus in lines 235–40.

Lines 181–204: These lines seem to offer more a Stoic ideal than a Christian one, though this does not greatly alter the conduct expected of the strong or virtuous man. The "high throne of immortality" (line 203) suggests fame rather than heaven but the difficult road to reach it sounds very like the Christian's narrow path to heaven.

Lines 223–40: Venus represents joy and beauty in the classical world, perhaps suggesting not so much a Christian or Stoic response to suffering as the idea that consolation may be found in art. The "high goal" of line 256 (Spanish 255) sounds neoplatonist and may derive from Garcilaso's friendship with Italian writers and humanists in Naples, or from Castiglione.

Lines 244–46: "Death loses its rights" in the temple of fame, because great men are not forgotten. Lines 250–52, on the other hand, suggest a Christian image of the purified soul ascending to heaven from purgatory and prepare us for the image of don Bernaldino looking down on the world from heaven.

Lines 253–55: Literally this passage begins "Do you think the fire … was different?" which sounds like an acknowledgment by Garcilaso that he is equating classical myth and Christian doctrine. On the other hand it may also have something to do with Ovid's slightly arch presentation of the death and apotheosis of Hercules (*Metamorphoses*, 9, 239–72).

Lines 256–57: "He for whom your heart gives out a thousand sighs" is of course don Bernaldino. The general message to don Fernando is "stop grieving because your brother is in heaven."

Line 261: "La dulce región del alegría" ("the sweet region of joy") is heaven or, in classical terms, the Elysian Fields.

Line 270: The lives of the grandfather, don Fadrique de Toledo, and the father, don García de Toledo, are described in the latter part of the second eclogue (not included here).

Lines 274–75: Their father died aged twenty-six in an earlier North African campaign.

Lines 276–79: I take this to imply that on earth you might seek compensation for your wounds by having vengeance on your enemy, but not in heaven, where your only reward is to show the wounds with pride.

Line 280: "He" is now don Bernaldino, not his father or grandfather.

Line 289: Rather confusingly, after just addressing Ferdinand on the subject of his brother and their father and grandfather, the poem switches and addresses Bernaldino and continues to do so until the end, although of course the compliment paid him in the concluding lines of the poem is also complimentary to Ferdinand, his grieving brother.

Lines 301–4: Fishes in the sea and wild boars on the mountain are found in a similar context in Virgil's Eclogue V, 76–78.

Line 307: The Spanish implies north by referring to Calisto, the nymph who was turned into the Great Bear.

ELEGY II

Lines 1–3: The "great Mantuan" is Virgil, who was born in Mantua, and the reference is to his epic poem the *Aeneid*. Aeneas rescued his father Anchises from the sack of Troy, but according to Virgil Anchises died when they reached Sicily and was buried there.

Lines 5–6: The "African Caesar" is the emperor Charles V: Garcilaso is comparing him to a Roman emperor and to Scipio Africanus, conqueror of Carthage (or to be precise, one of the two Scipios who at different dates won victories over Carthage). (See Sonnet XXXV and comments in Helgerson.)

Lines 7–9: These lines have sometimes been taken as referring to booty from the sack of Tunis, but in the context of different parties squabbling it seems likely to be a question of rewards and honors in the Emperor's service.

Lines 16–18: Garcilaso's concern (or so he says here) is to find a middle way between showing he is interested in his own profit and appearing hypocritical in proclaiming his disregard for it. This kind of aristocratic indifference to gain is exactly what we would expect from him. The impression is reinforced by what is surely understatement for the sake of emphasis in the last line of the tercet: "un poco mas que aquellos me levanto," literally, "I raise myself a little higher than them."

Lines 19–21: My version has "from north to south" for the sake of the sound: the Spanish does however imply horses with "a la otra via vuelven...la rienda," "they turn the reins the other way."

Lines 22–24: It would surely be wrong to think this expresses a real mistake in composition or failure to control his pen. Humorous pretence seems to underlie the expression "me voy mi paso a paso," "I am going step-by-step."

Lines 25–27: There are ambiguities here. The link to the preceding lines is clear: he is changing the subject, getting back to his original intention. But what is that intention? Where is it he will be heading (as he always has)? Boscan is supposed to know, but do we? Ostensibly yes, it is love and the suffering love brings, a subject that was licensed by the Petrarchan fashion he is following. But by not spelling this out he leaves it open for us to suppose a wider theme.

Line 27: "Siempre ha llevado y lleva Garcilaso," "Garcilaso has always taken and takes"—this linking of the same verb in two tenses occurs elsewhere in Garcilaso. It seems mainly emphatic.

Lines 28–30: More difficulties: not every edition places a comma at the end of line 28, and it has been read as "dense forest *of* diversities." However, this reading seems to leave "me sostengo" somewhat unsupported and unclear. I prefer to see "monte espesso," "dense mountain or forest" (the word "monte" can mean any wild terrain) standing alone as a periphrasis for "this life" or "the world," and take the following phrase as "de diversidades me sostengo," "I sustain myself on diversities," which I assume to be something similar to his famous statement in Eclogue III that he alternates between the sword and the pen. I have to admit though that my line 28 is driven by the eye rhyme.

Lines 31–36: The meaning is straightforward, but very hard to express concisely. I find "shuttle between [the muses and my work]" in Ann Cruz's essay, which gets the meaning well, but to my ear sounds too modern. I have erred similarly myself in line 36 with "take it easy," but there I wanted to stress what seemed like Castiglione's *sprezzatura* (a kind of nonchalance, or "graceful and nonchalant spontaneity," in George Bull's translation). I do not think Garcilaso is downgrading the muses: it is a pretence. In this poem Garcilaso moves between apparent carelessness and intense seriousness.

Lines 37–39: The land of the Siren or Parthenope is Naples, and already in antiquity it had this reputation for fun and games.

Lines 40–42: Presumably Garcilaso has a lover in Naples, from whom he has been separated during the North African campaign.

Lines 43–45: Jealousy.

Lines 46–69: The comparison of absence to pouring water on a fire to extinguish it has been described as *cancioneril* and as such, I think, implicitly criticized. There is no doubt that it distances the emotion of jealousy and calms it by objectifying it. But that in a way is the point: just as a little water does not extinguish the fire (of love), so intellectual analysis cannot reduce its power to hurt.

Lines 70–93: These tortured lines contrast with the clarity of the preceding water and fire metaphor. Garcilaso claims he is a special case because absence does not cause him to forget, but increases his suffering. This is reasonable, he says, because he was always destined to plunge himself into love's fire. There can be no end therefore to his suffering, no reason for hope.

Line 80: "Absence" in this context is absence of or from the lover.

Lines 88–90: More literally, "This fear persecutes hope and oppresses and weakens the great desire with which my eyes follow their pleasure," "con que mis ojos van de su holganza," one of Garcilaso's wonderfully suggestive phrases. I believe it refers to a state of depression in which even what should give delight fails to do so.

Lines 91–93: He sees nothing but the pain that splits his heart, and fights with it and with himself. Garcilaso refers elsewhere (Eclogue II, and at the end of this poem) to a sense of being divided from or in himself.

Line 97: There is a slight ambiguity in the expression "que tiene que hacer" that might be expressed as "what has he/she/it to do with" or "what must he/she do about." In this instance, the first seems more suitable.

Lines 100–108: Is the death wish expressed here just a rhetorical gesture? Is it because he has no time to devote to his lover and thus cannot prevent her unfaithfulness, or does it express some deeper disgust with his military service?

Lines 109–11: The question about where his fear takes him, "¿donde me transporta y enajena?" echoes the question in line 22. The answer, that it is a place full of misery and shame, recalls the terrifying place, "aquel lugar tan espantable," of Sonnet XXX. Some of the power of these nightmare places comes from their vagueness.

Lines 112–20: He is delving into his own psychology. The unconfirmed fear seems as bad as the reality. And yet, if he knew the reality, and it is what he fears it is, he would look back on the time when he could still doubt and hope as a happier one, and wish that he still had only an imagined betrayal to deal with.

Lines 121–44: Perhaps there is some justification for applying the term "sincere" to Garcilaso, not as an unprovable description of his love, but because of the point he makes here about the need to face the truth and the deadly attractiveness of self-deception.

Lines 145–56: These gloomy thoughts are abruptly interrupted with the word "You," as he considers the happiness of his friend, Boscán, married now and no longer serving the emperor but living at home in Barcelona.

Lines 151–52: The flame that caused Troy to be burnt down was the love between Helen and Paris.

Line 156: More literally this is "for the pure shining calms the wind," a beautiful image for the love he envies in his friend's secure married life, so different from his own, and an echo of Sonnet XXIII, line 4.

Lines 157–59: Yet another welcoming of death, followed by a long exposition of the difficulty of maintaining hope. Here "mercenary" (line 157) is surely metaphorical and expresses weariness or self-disgust.

Line 168: Compare the last two lines of Sonnet XXIII.

Lines 175–77: Libya was conventionally associated in antiquity with poisonous snakes.

Line 191: "Apurarse" can mean both to be purified and to be troubled, but I think the context gives more weight to the latter meaning. I hope that "mortified" retains a degree of ambiguity.

EPISTLE TO BOSCÁN

Line 10: The word I translate as "carelessness" is "descuido," which is also the word Boscán used to translate Castiglione's "sprezzatura" (in George Bull's modern English version, "nonchalance").

Line 13: I take "cuanto a lo primero" to mean the first of the two advantages he has mentioned (in lines 4–5) of writing to friends: the ease of finding a subject. He will simply begin with the journey.

Lines 15–16: At the end of the letter his reader will know how far he has travelled, because he will learn where the letter is written from. The poem imitates a letter, and ends with the sender's address. But note that this is a kind of fiction. It is not really a letter and there is nothing to prevent the writer of the poem from saying where he is at the start.

Lines 30–64: Garcilaso is analyzing friendship here and speaks of its having different parts. Editors say this is derived from Aristotle's Nichomachean Ethics, where Aristotle divides friendship into different kinds: friendships of good people, friendships based on utility, friendships based on pleasure. The best and most enduring are those between good people because they wish good to the other for the other's own sake.

Line 30: This sounds to me like a reference to a particular person, rather than a generalization. I assume he has Aristotle in mind, though of course there are plenty of others who wrote on friendship.

Lines 36–41: I think this formulation, which he seeks to explain in lines 51–65, is Garcilaso's own. I am not sure whether his introduction of "love" ("amor") rather than "friendship" is significant. He may just intend, like Aristotle, to distinguish a higher form of friendship from that based on utility or pleasure.

Lines 53–54: This bond of love definitely unites both their hearts.

Line 57: There is a slight doubt here about the meaning of "el amor." Helgerson takes it as referring to love in general, but for me, despite the following comma, it seems to fit better as a reference to his love in particular, the love he gives when he has only the other's good in mind, because Garcilaso's purpose here is to analyze his own motives. There is a problem with the syntax. A very literal translation into English produces a tautology: "But love, which . . . , is a great reason why [it? love?] should be held by me in greater esteem than all the rest." The problem, briefly, is connected with the fact that in English a noun in initial position is generally both grammatical subject and topic of the sentence (one can separate the indication of topic from grammatical subject by saying, "As for love, it is . . ."). We could take "es gran razon" in line 60 as an impersonal expression: "there is a great reason why it should be . . ." but this still leaves the first part of the sentence without a complement. I believe this supports my view that Garcilaso's intention was to describe the *kind* of love he has in mind (the love that *perhaps* brings benefit to the other person, in this case Boscán) and go on to say it is reasonable for him to esteem it above all other kinds, because it is unselfishly given, and to give is better than to receive. I have followed Rivers and others in line 58 because it seems to make better sense to have a comma after "si hay alguna," making it parenthetical.

Line 66: The sudden change of subject is characteristic of friendly communication when speakers or writers feel they are becoming too serious and remedy the situation with humor. We are surely not expected to believe this is really an apology or an expression of real shame.

Line 81: Their friend Durall was apparently rather fat.

Lines 84–85: The tomb of Petrarch's Laura had recently been located in Avignon.

ECLOGUE I

Lines 4–6: I cannot believe Garcilaso was totally unaware of the comic effect of these sheep. There is precedent however in Virgil's eighth eclogue.

Lines 7–14: The poem is addressed to don Pedro de Toledo of the house of Alba, viceroy of Naples, Garcilaso's immediate employer.

Lines 11–12: This actually refers to Naples, a colony of Spain, but since it is governed by a member of the house of Alba, I suppose it can be a realm of Alba. Some editors punctuate differently, reading "Albano" as the name of the addressee, rather than an adjective qualifying "estado."

Line 27: Literally, "before I am consumed."

Line 28: The Spanish contrasts "faltar," to be lacking, with "sobrar," to be in excess, or in this case to stand out or outdo. To die before he has adequately extolled don Pedro would show him as "lacking" toward someone who is always "exceeding." There is also the sense of defaulting on a due payment, which leads conveniently to the mention of debt in the next stanza. It is difficult to express the full sense in English, but my anachronistic "sell you short" is an attempt to alert the reader to this complication.

Lines 38–40: The "ivy" is himself, as a writer of pastoral poetry, not epic, which would be associated with the laurel of victory. He is more or less saying, "Sorry, can't write you an epic today, I don't have time." Also, of course, ivy, like the poet, needs support. I have changed "praise" ("loores") to "fame" to remove a possible ambiguity: the praise other people give to don Pedro, not don Pedro's praise for Garcilaso.

Lines 43–49: Similar descriptions of sunrise can be found in Virgil, in Eclogue VIII for example, but the Arcadian setting probably owes more to Sannazaro.

Lines 58–60: The pairing of hot and cold, fire and snow, is common in Garcilaso, as it is in his Italian models.

Lines 109–10: The sinister crow was really a crow seen on the left-hand side ("sinistra" = left), which the Romans considered an ill omen.

Lines 121–25: Clearly the changed course of the river corresponds to the inconstant lover. I have translated "curso enajenado" two lines later as "perverted" rather than just "diverted," to suggest an accusing tone. As well as "changed," "enajenado" can mean mad or out of one's mind.

Line 137: There was a custom mentioned from Roman times of planting elms with vines to give them support.

Lines 155—67: These lines are often taken as referring to Isabel Freyre's having married someone Garcilaso considered not good enough for her. However, similar (but not the same) examples of impossibilities are found in Virgil, Eclogue VIII, lines 26—28 and 52—56, where jealousy is also the topic.

Lines 169—80: The jilted lover boasting of his possessions and finding himself not ugly appears in Virgil's Eclogue II, lines 19—25, and a generation or two after Garcilaso this figure is taken up by Góngora in the comic boasting of his giant, Polyphemus.

Lines 189—93: More peasant boasting, deriving from Virgil, but these are Spanish sheep that undertake "trashumación," the migration between winter and summer pastures.

Lines 235—38: This abdication of responsibility by the narrator follows Virgil, Eclogue VIII, lines 63—64.

Lines 239—52: Nemoroso's lament begins with what seems like a celebration of life but we soon learn that his joy is a thing of the past. Once again, the contrast between past joy and present unhappiness.

Line 258: "Elisa" is a near-anagram of Isabel.

Line 260: Usually it is the *thread* of life that is cut by the fates, three sisters who spin and cut it, but here Garcilaso definitely speaks of a cloth.

Lines 294—95: Literally, "alone, helpless, / blind, without light, in a dark prison."

Lines 308—9: There is a similar idea in sonnet XI, where the lover's (Apollo's) tears cause the tree (Daphne), which is their cause, to grow faster.

Lines 310—21: This nightmare stanza is similar in tone to Sonnet XXXII and also recalls the "place where fear prevails," "aquel lugar tan espantable," of Sonnet XXX on jealousy, and the "place full of misery and shame" in Elegy II, line 111. The end recalls Sonnet XXV but is calmer and more hopeful: the eclogue is gradually, haltingly moving toward a serene close.

Lines 352—63: The return to the present and the physical detail of the lock of hair intensifies the pathos.

Lines 364—65: This momentary relief is the kind of psychological detail Garcilaso likes to record. It adds poignancy to the next stanza's vision of Elisa dying.

Line 371: Lucina is also Diana, in her role of birth goddess. Isabel died in childbirth in 1534.

Lines 376–81: The goddess Diana was usually hunting, but she also found time to fall in love with the shepherd Endymion, for whom she arranged perpetual sleep, so that as Moon she could come out each night to embrace him.

Line 400: The third heaven is the domain of Venus.

Lines 408–421: The action began at dawn (lines 43–45) and calm now returns with the ending of the day. The shepherds awake "as if from a dream." The same word, "recordar," usually "to remember," was used by the earlier poet Jorge Manrique for the kind of awakening that leads men to repent of their sins before they die.

Eclogue II

Lines 4–9: The day when Camila learnt of his love and fled from him—as we shall hear later.

Lines 10–18: The contrast between beautiful surroundings and mental torment is a recurrent theme (compare Song III).

Lines 25–30: Albanio's argument with himself shows Garcilaso's design to dramatize the action.

Lines 38–76: This song, deriving from the *beatus ille* of Horace, had an important influence on later Spanish golden age poetry: both the form and the substance are found again in the poetry of Fray Luís de León and Góngora.

Line 61: Literally, he hates it so much that "he still does not think he is safe from it," or one might say, he simply cannnot do enough to distance himself from it.

Lines 80–85: These lines are variously punctuated in different editions. The punctuation in Navarro Tomás seems to me the more logical.

Lines 110–12: In a true dramatic text a practiced hand would later introduce this "someone" into the action. Garcilaso names him in line 128, but does not give him even a walk-on part. The way of referring to him here, however, suggests that Salicio's soliloquy is really an address to the audience.

Lines 113–21: Albanio's confusion on waking from a dream foreshadows the madness he later will fall into.

Line 117: The "ivory gate" is the gate of false dreams, in classical mythology.

Line 128 (Spanish 129): Galafrón has to be referred to by name because Salicio is now speaking to Albanio, who doubtless knows him. Clearly Garcilaso is trying for some degree of realism. Galafrón is again spoken of near the end of the poem, as likely not to have lit the fire yet in the shepherds' hut. This is all reasonable, but no further use is made of Galafrón. If we can speak of dramatic technique here, it is still rudimentary.

Lines 134–38: This could be autobiographical, a reference to Garcilaso's diplomatic missions that took him away from Naples.

Lines 431–45: Once more the spring is an essential feature of this special place, apparently a cool and safe refuge from the midday heat. Góngora also describes such a place in his *Polifemo*.

Lines 467–84: The incident is improbable. But this is a fairy tale world, where chaste brother-and-sister love and lust coexist and can become confused.

Line 790: After the romantic introduction, the violence of Albanio's behavior comes as a surprise. But is it perhaps the natural concomitant of his earlier timidity and romanticism?

Line 795: Further evidence that Albanio does not see Camila as a living independent person: he thinks he may lose his inhibitions when she is sleeping, because it is as if she were dead.

Lines 823–25: Camila's perception seems very modern: we almost have the basis of a feminist theme here. There is a definite attempt by Garcilaso to enter the minds or psychology of his characters.

Line 827: Camila reminds Albanio and the reader that the fountain or spring was both the setting and the instrument on the occasion when he made known to her what was in his mind.

Line 850: When Camila speaks of the loss of her gold pin the mood swings toward comedy.

Line 886: Albanio's madness is characterized by his feeling separated from himself, floating above the world as a disembodied spirit.

ECLOGUE III

Line 2: He is probably addressing doña Maria Osorio Pimentel, wife of the viceroy.

Line 13: "Roca," in Italian "rocca," a fortress or prison.

Lines 23–24: To fill out the line I have had to elaborate slightly with "rips and tears," but there is a degree of redundancy in the Spanish too, with "quita," "takes away," and "arrebata," "snatches."

Line 38: I think this is ambiguous and I have deliberately retained the ambiguity in my version. It can mean that there is scarcely anyone who opposes the fury of Mars, but it might also mean that it is hard to resist joining in, or difficult to maintain an individual stance and remain uninfluenced by violence.

Line 39: More literally, "I stole this brief amount of time."

Lines 51–52: There is redundancy in the original: "I give you what I can and what I have given, by your receiving it, I grow rich."

Lines 57–68: Much has been written by other poets and novelists about the river Tagus as it hurries through the gorge surrounding the southern half of Toledo and slows as it widens into the plain. Modern visitors may not find such luxuriant growth along its banks, but most people will find Garcilaso's enthusiasm justified by the view of the river when they look down from the old city's terraces or by the sight of packed houses, towers, and domes viewed from the opposite hill.

Lines 79–80: The onomatopoeia in the line about the bees is much quoted as an example of Góngora's musical quality.

Line 128: Orpheus.

Lines 153–60: Much of the detail is taken from Ovid's *Metamorphoses*, 1:495–596, in particular Apollo's concern that Daphne may injure herself in her precipitous flight. Daphne is also the subject of Sonnet XIII. But here the moral about the thwarted lover adding to his own suffering by making the tree grow with his tears is missing.

Lines 189–90: This kiss of life was parodied by Góngora in his *Pyramus and Thisbe*.

Lines 197–216: Toledo. Line 200 suggests that for all his internationalism Garcilaso remained strongly attached to his native place.

Line 230: Most editions have "degollada," a word with meanings that range from "slaughtered" to "strangled" or "beheaded," but there has been controversy over this at least since the sixteenth-century editor El Brocense found it repulsive and said he was sure Garcilaso had written *igualada*, which would mean something like "lying on the ground," or possibly "shrouded." Support based on the idea that Garcilaso was following Ovid can be found in an article by B. Morros on the Centro Virtual Cervantes Web site. I have fudged the issue somewhat because I think the image of the dead swan is sufficiently powerful anyway to suggest the destruction of beauty and innocence. The more violent alternative might be:

> In a dappled place beside the stream she lay,
> her throat cut, lodged in a leafy bower.

Line 241: Elisa, it has often been pointed out, is nearly an anagram of Isabel. Lusitania is Portugal, so there is good reason to assume a reference to Isabel Freyre here. It has been argued, however, that Nemoroso represents not Garcilaso but his friend Boscán, or even Isabel's husband, Antonio de Fonseca.

Lines 289–90: Here, as in several other places, the opening lines of the stanza seem to repeat part of the close of the preceding stanza, giving a curious echo effect and perhaps a reminiscence of oral narration.

Lines 305–76: The idea of these competing songs is from Virgil. They are built around contrasts: sweet/bitter, calm/stormy, and so on.

Line 323: Favonius and Zephyr are Roman and Greek names for the warm winds of spring.

Line 372: There is another touch of realism when the shepherds start to move a little faster, "con paso un poco mas apresurado." For all his pastoral stylization, Garcilaso apparently seeks imaginative involvement with his subject.

Lines 375–76: More literally, the foam covers the water as they dive in.

Appendix B

In his first paragraph Garcilaso speaks of Boscán's objection to "romancing" books—turning them into romance or the vernacular. I am not sure what he (or Boscán) would mean by this, so "vulgarize" is just a guess.

Likewise, in the third paragraph I do not know what the books "that speak of killing" are, though I imagine them to be the chivalrous romances we are familiar with mainly from *Don Quijote*.

Selected Bibliography

Barnard, Mary E. "Garcilaso's Poetics of Subversion in the Orpheus Tapestry." *PMLA* 102 (1987): 316–25.

Castiglione, B. *The Book of the Courtier*. Translated by George Bull. London: Penguin, 2003.

Cruz, Anne J. "Self-Fashioning in Spain: Garcilaso de la Vega." *Romanic Review* 83 (1992): 517–38.

———. "Arms Versus Letters: The Poetics of War and the Career of the Poet in Early Modern Spain." In *European Literary Careers: The Author from Antiquity to the Renaissance*, edited by Patrick Cheney and Frederick A. de Armas. Toronto: University of Toronto Press, 2002.

Elliott, J. H. *Imperial Spain, 1469–1716*. London: Penguin, 1985.

Garcilaso de la Vega. *Obras de Garcilaso de la Vega*. Edited by T. Navarro Tomás. Madrid: Ediciones de "La Lectura," 1911.

———. *Poesía castellana completa*. Edited by Consuelo Burrell. Madrid: Ediciones Cátedra, 2006.

———. *Poesías castellanas completas*. Edited by Elias L. Rivers. Madrid: Clásicos Castalia, 1979.

———. *Poesía completa*. Edited by Juan Francisco Alcina. Madrid: Colección Austral, 1998.

———. *Poesías completas*. Edited by Angel L. Prieto de Paula. Madrid: Editorial Castalia, 1989.

Graf, Eric C. "From Scipio to Nero to the Self: The Exemplary Politics of Stoicism in Garcilaso de la Vega's Elegies." *PMLA* 116 (2001): 1316–33.

Greenblatt, S. *Renaissance Self-Fashioning*. Chicago: University of Chicago Press, 1980. Revised edition published in 2005.

Heiple, Daniel. *Garcilaso de la Vega and the Italian Renaissance*. University Park: Pennsylvania State University Press, 1994.

Helgerson, R. *A Sonnet from Carthage*. Philadelphia: University of
Pennsylvania Press, 2007.

Lapesa, Rafael. *La trayectoria poética de Garcilaso*. Madrid: Editorial
Revista de Occidente, 1968.

Murphy, Martin. *Blanco White: Self-banished Spaniard*. New Haven: Yale
University Press, 1989.

Navarrete, Ignacio. *Orphans of Petrarch: Poetry and Theory in the Italian
Renaissance*. Berkeley: University of California Press, 1994.

Ovid. *Metamorphoses*. Translated by David Raeburn. London: Penguin,
2004.

Rivers, Elias. "Garcilaso's Poetry: Between Love Affairs and Annota-
tions." *MLN* 115 (2000): 355–66.

Smith, Paul Julian. *Writing in the Margin: Spanish Literature of the Golden
Age*. Oxford: Clarendon Press; Oxford University Press, 1988.

Vaquero Serrano, Maria del Carmen. *Garcilaso: Poeta del amor, caballero
de la guerra*. Madrid: Editorial Espasa Calpe, 2002.

Virgil. *The Aeneid*. Translated by Robert Fagles. London: Penguin, 2007.

———. *The Eclogues*. Translated by Guy Lee. London: Penguin, 1984.

WEB SITES

www.cvc.cervantes.es/actcult/garcilaso (Instituto Cervantes).

www.garcilaso.org (*La Página de Garcilaso en internet promovida por la
Asociación de amigos de Garcilaso*).

Index of Titles and First Lines

¡Oh hado esecutivo en mis dolores, 44
O fate, so active to promote my troubles, 45
O sweet mementoes, unfortunately found, 35
Pensando que el camino iba derecho, 40
Señor Boscán, for one who takes such pleasure, 111
Señor Boscán, quien tanto gusto tiene, 110
Si de mi baja lira, 66
Slender nymphs who dwell within the river, 37
Suspicion, how you occupy my sad, 47
Sospechas, que en mi triste fantasía, 46
That pure and honorable sense of duty, 181
Thinking that the road I took was straight, 41
To love you must be a fault, 207
When I stop to view my situation, 31
While colors of the lily and the rose, 43
With the gentle lapping, 61
Your countenance is written in my soul, 33